CUT TIME

CUT TIME

An Education at the Fights

Carlo Rotella

HOUGHTON MIFFLIN COMPANY

BOSTON · NEW YORK   2003

For information about permission to reproduce selections
from this book, write Permissions, Houghton Mifflin Company,
215 Park Avenue South, New York, New York 10003.

Visit our Web site: www.houghtonmifflinbooks.com.

Library of Congress Cataloging-in-Publication Data

Rotella, Carlo, 1964–
Cut time : an education at the fights / Carlo Rotella.
p. cm.
ISBN 0-618-14533-8
1. Boxing. 2. Rotella, Carlo, 1964– I. Title.
GV1133.R69 2003
796.83—dc21 2002191286
Printed in the United States of America

Book design by Robert Overholtzer

QUM 10 9 8 7 6 5 4 3 2 1

Portions of this book previously appeared, in somewhat
different form, in the *Washington Post Magazine,*
The American Scholar, DoubleTake, and *Transition.*

For Jim Fisher

Up the hill and down the hill

We both come to punish the person. The difference is I think about some of the things I want to throw. I don't throw them wild and out of context. My punches have meaning.

— Terronn Millett, shortly before fighting Arturo Gatti, who knocked him out

Everything in life is mental. I came back and won a world title after I broke my neck because I'm mental. I won five world titles because I'm mental. Same reason I'll bring this belt home to my parents.

— Vinny Paz, shortly before fighting Eric Lucas, who won by decision

Contents

Introduction: At Ringside   1

1   Halfway   17

2   Cut Time   31

3   Mismatches   53

4   An Appetite for Hitting   83

5   Out of Order   111

6   The Switch   135

7   The Distance   163

8   Bidness   185

9   Hurt   205

Acknowledgments   221

CUT TIME

Introduction

At Ringside

Ringside comes into being whenever the hitting starts
and both combatants know how to do it. There is almost
always a place on the margins of a fight for interested
observers; most fights, even those between drunks in the
street, would not happen without them. In the narrow
sense, though, ringside requires a ring. Inside a ring, fighting can come under the shaping influence of the rules,
traditions, and institutions of boxing. The fight world is
grounded in relatively few pieces of real estate — the International Boxing Hall of Fame in Canastota, New York, for
instance, or the Blue Horizon in Philadelphia — but it also
floats across the landscape, touching down and coalescing
in material form when a casino puts up a ring for a night of
boxing, or when a trainer rents a storefront and fills it with

punching bags and a couple of duct-taped situp mats and a ring for sparring. When the gym loses its lease or when the casino has to clear its hall the next day for a Legends of Doo-Wop concert, the fight world packs up and moves on, traveling light. A ring is just a medium-sized truckful of metal struts, plywood flooring, foam padding, canvas, ropes, cables, and miscellaneous parts; it takes only a couple of hours for a competent crew to assemble it or break it down. While the ring is set up it creates ringside — and the possibility of learning something.

There are lessons to be learned at ringside. Close to but apart from both the action and the paying audience watching it, you see in two directions at once: into the cleared fighting space inside the ropes, and outward at the wide world spreading messily outside the ropes. You must learn specialized boxing knowledge to make sense of what you see in the ring, but the consequences of those lessons extend far beyond boxing. The deeper you go into the fights, the more you may discover about things that would seem at first blush to have nothing to do with boxing. Lessons in spacing and leverage, or in holding part of oneself in reserve even when hotly engaged, are lessons not only in how one boxer reckons with another but also in how one person reckons with another. The fights teach many such lessons — about the virtues and limits of craft, about the need to impart meaning to hard facts by enfolding them in stories and spectacle, about getting hurt and getting old, about distance and intimacy, and especially about education itself: boxing conducts an endless workshop in the teaching and learning of knowledge with consequences.

A serious education in boxing, for an observer as well as a fighter, entails regular visits to the gym, where the show-biz distractions of fight night recede and matters of craft take precedence. Gyms are places of repetition and permutation. A fighter refines a punch by throwing it over and over in the mirror and then at a bag and then at an opponent. A short guy and a tall guy in the sparring ring work out their own solutions to the ancient problem of fighting somebody taller or shorter than oneself. Everybody there, no matter how deeply caught up in his own business, remains alert to the instructive value of other people's labors. My first and best boxing school has been the Larry Holmes Training Center, a long, low, shedlike building facing the railroad tracks and the river on Canal Street in Easton, Pennsylvania. Holmes, the gym's owner and principal pugilist, was the best heavyweight in the world in the late 1970s and early 1980s, and he had an extended run as undisputed champion. He has been retiring and unretiring since then, fighting on through his forties and past fifty. His afternoon training sessions at the gym have allowed younger fighters to work alongside a master, and interested observers to watch.

Holmes, the last of the twentieth century's great heavyweight stylists, practices the manly art of self-defense as it used to be taught. A big, prickly fellow with a no-nonsense workingman's body and an oddly planed head that seems to deflect incoming shots like a tank's turret, he has prospered through diligent application of the principle of defense with bad intentions. He puts technique before musculature, good sense before crowd-pleasing drama, perseverance before rage. Boxing is unnatural: instinct does not teach you to move toward a hard hitter, rather than away from him, to cut down his leverage; you do not instinctively bring your hand back to blocking position after you punch with it; almost nobody feels a natural urge to stay on his feet when badly hurt by a blow, or to get up within ten seconds of having been knocked down. Even after a lifetime of fighting, a boxer has to reinforce and relearn good habits in training. Sitting on one of the banged-up folding chairs arranged at ringside in Holmes's gym, you could pick up some of those habits — or at least an appreciation of them — by watching him at work.

My education as a ringsider probably began at the first school I ever attended, the Ancona Montessori School. I spent the better part of two years there banging a green plastic Tyrannosaurus rex into a blue plastic Triceratops (and then putting them away where they belonged, which is what Montessori schools and well-run gyms are all about), absorbing the widely applicable groundline truth that styles make fights. The gangly T. rex had to risk being gored in order to bite; the squatty Triceratops had to risk being bitten in order to gore; and T. rex had to force the action like a challenger, rather than the undisputed champion among dinosaurs he was supposed to be: he needed meat, while Triceratops could get by on shrubs. Among nonextinct fighters, I knew who Muhammad Ali was, but he was mostly a face and a voice, like Fred Flintstone. The first boxer I recognized as a boxer was Larry Holmes, who was sizing up and solving one contender after another, sometimes on television, when I was in high school. Holmes, part T. rex and part Triceratops, had the first boxing style I could see as such. Circling and jabbing, he wore through the other man's fight like a toxic solvent. A little more than a decade after leaving high school — having gone on to college and graduate school and a first teaching job at Lafayette College, which overlooks Easton from the steep remove of College Hill — I went for a walk to explore the town and found my way down Canal Street to Holmes's classroom.

I am not saying, as Ishmael says of a whale ship in *Moby-Dick,* that a boxing gym was my Yale College and my Harvard. I go there to watch, not to train. I'm inclined by temperament to look blankly at a potential fistfighting opponent until he gets bored and goes away, and I'm built physically to flee predators with bounding strides and sudden shifts of direction. Yale and Harvard and other schools like them have, in fact, been my Yale College and my Harvard. You can get an education at ringside, but you also bring your own education to ringside.

I'm currently in something like the thirtieth grade of a formal education that began at the Ancona Montessori School, and somewhere along the way I picked up the habit of research. Visits to ringside and conversations with fight people inspire visits to the archive to pursue context and understanding. The archive of boxing includes a library of edifying and sometimes elegant writing that reaches from the latest typo-riddled issue of *Boxing Digest* all the way back to a one-punch KO in book 23 of the *Iliad,* but it also includes many thousands of fights on film and videotape. Seeing a bout from ringside sends me to the VCR with a stack of tapes to study the styles and stories of the combatants, or to consider analogous fights informed by a similar principle: bomber versus tactician, old head versus young lion, showboat versus plumber. I get the tapes in the mail from Gary, an ascetic in outer Wisconsin, and from Mike, a scholar in Kansas with a good straight left who sounds just like a young Howard Cosell (except that Mike knows what he's talking about). Gary and Mike trade tapes with a motley network of connoisseur collectors, fistic philosophes, and aggression freaks who convene on the Internet to argue over such arcana as whether John L. Sullivan could have coped with Roy Jones Jr.'s handspeed. If the tape-traders' network can also provide a copy of a bout I attended (not always possible, since I often cover tank-town cards that escape the notice even of regional cable and video bootleggers), I review it to see what cameras and microphones might have caught that I did not.

Even if it begins in the gym, a ringside education has to reckon with television, which has dominated the fights since it rose to power in the 1950s. That's when boxing began to become an esoteric electronic spectacle rather than a regular feature of neighborhood life (and that's when A. J. Liebling was moved to write a definitive and already nostalgic defense of seeing a fight in person, "Boxing with the Naked Eye"). From ringside, you can see the signs of television's dominance. Bouts begin when the network's schedule requires them to begin; extra-bright lights make everything appear to be in too sharp focus. Announcers, producers, and technicians have a roped-off section of ringside to themselves. Camera operators with shoulder mounts stand outside the ropes on the ring apron, trailing cables behind them as they follow the action. They interfere with the crowd's view of the fighters, but the inconvenience makes a sort of sense: a few hundred or a few thousand attendees put up with a partially blocked view so that millions, potentially, can see everything.

Not only does TV money dictate the fight world's priorities, TV technology also promises to turn your living room into ringside. These days, cameras and microphones can bring spectators at home closer to the action than would a ringside seat. When you watch a fight on television, a corner mike lets you horn in on a trainer's whispered final instruction to his fighter before the bell, and you can see the fighter's features distort and ripple in slow motion from three different angles as he gets hit with the combination the trainer warned him about. Some part of me knows that this is all deeply intimate and therefore none of my business, even as I pause the tape and then rewind it so I can write down exactly what the trainer said and note the precise sequence of punches.

But television hides as much as it reveals. For one thing, it tells you what to watch. It does not let you turn around to look at the crowd, whose surging presence you can hear, and smell, and feel on your skin at ringside. It does not allow you to look away from the terrible mismatch in the ring to watch for flashes of shame behind the boxing commissioners' impassivity. It also muffles the perception of leverage and distance, the sense of consequences, available at ringside. You often can't tell how hard the punches are; occasionally, you can't tell what is happening at all. After eleven Zapruderine replays, you still ask, Was that a hard shot or a glancing blow? Did it knock him down or did he stumble? Returning to a fight on tape can fill in or correct my understanding of what I saw in person from ringside, and I'm grateful that the boxing archive on videotape has allowed me to see a century's worth of fights that I could never have seen in person, but I don't try to score a fight unless I was there in person. I thought John Ruiz was robbed when judges gave the decision to Evander Holyfield in their first fight, but I only saw it on television, so I can't be sure. Had I been at ringside, I might have concluded that Holyfield hit so much harder than Ruiz that he deserved to win rounds in which he landed fewer blows.

The apparatus of television is not always equal to the task of connecting action to its meaningful context. Television seems to get you close enough to see almost everything and taste the flying sweat, but its appeal lies primarily in cool distance. There's a basketball game on one channel, a tragic romance on the next, a ten-round bloodbath on the next, and in each case the camera does the equivalent of following the ball, tracing broad emotions and basic narrative contours. For reasons that have as much to do with business as technology, television can't or won't capture the off-the-ball struggle of four against five to create or advantageous angles to the basket, or the nearness of another sleeping body in a bed, or the slight changes in distance a smart defensive fighter constantly makes between himself and his opponent to neutralize the other man's developing punches.

That leaves it up to the on-air announcers to connect action to meaningful context. Talking from bell to bell, they model and parody the processes of education at the fights. When the HBO crew works a bout, for instance, Jim Lampley divides his time between describing the action and mock-crunching the opaque CompuBox numbers that purport to quantify the bout's progress. Larry Merchant, the professorial one, offers boxing lore and the occasional historical or literary reference. Mostly, though, he makes a smelling-a-bad-smell face I associate with French public intellectuals and explains that the guy who isn't winning is the more egregious example of how men are no longer men in this debased age. George Foreman, who used to hurt people for a living, is the most sympathetic to the fighters, but wildly erratic and often plain wrong in his commentary. I'm always in some suspense as to how long he can hold back from expressing his obsessive fear of being touched on the chest: "That's how you take a man's *power.*" When moonlighting active boxers like Roy Jones Jr. or Oscar De La Hoya sit in on a broadcast, they seem to be running their thoughts past an internal Marketing Department before articulating them. By the time the profound and useful things they could be telling us about boxing have made it back from Marketing, thoroughly revised, all that's left is press-release haiku: "Well, Jim, I think they're / Both great, great competitors / And very fine men." I always start out rooting for the announcers to break free of the bonds of the form — they are, after all, offering ways to get something out of boxing, which is what I'm doing in this book — but I soon end up wishing they would shut up so I can hear as well as see the electronic facsimile of the fight.

They don't shut up, though, and anyway, television is a weak substitute for being there, so I go to the fights. It's better to sit close, and nobody sits closer than ringsiders (who feel the petty little pleasure of having the big spenders and celebrities seated just behind them), so I cover fights for magazines and newspapers. I pick up my credentials at the press table, hang the laminated badge around my neck, and make my way to ringside. At a local club fight, nobody stops me to check my badge; I find an empty press seat at the long table abutting the ring apron and say hello to other regulars. In Massachusetts, where I live now, that means Charlie Ross, the gentle old-timer who writes for the apoplectic North End paper, the *Post-Gazette;* Mike Nosky, a mailman who moonlights for RealBoxing.com and briefly managed a cruiserweight out of Worcester named Roy "House of" Payne; and Skeeter McClure, who won a gold medal as a light middleweight in the 1960 Olympics, and who used to head the state boxing commission before a new governor's cronies squeezed him out. At a casino or a big arena like Madison Square Garden, ushers and security guards look over my badge at checkpoints controlling access to ringside, where several rows of tables and seats have been set up to accommodate a small mob of functionaries, reporters from all over, and television people.

In a club or at the Garden, the prefight scene is always fundamentally the same. The ring girls, in bathing gear and high heels, have draped other people's jackets around their shoulders to keep warm. Guys in suit and tie from the state commission walk back and forth with great conviction, glad-handing and trying to look busy. The referee for the first bout bounces lightly on the ropes to test the tension, then straightens his bow tie. (My favorite local referee is Eddie Fitzgerald, a smiling gentleman with flowing white hair who breaks fighters out of a clinch as if making room to step between them to order a highball. He taps them briskly on the shoulder as if to say, "*Gentlemen, there's no need to fight*.") The promoter walks by, flush and tight, usually managing to make his priciest clothes look like a forty-dollar rental. He stops to rub important people's necks and shoulders; he points across the room with a wink or a grin to those who don't merit a stop; he looks over the crowd filling up the hall, pressing in on ringside from all around. Cornermen and old fighters stand in clusters, talking about the time Bobby D got headbutted by that animal out of Scranton. Photographers check their equipment and load film, like infantry preparing to repel an assault. Print and on-line reporters hang around gossiping. Some of the deadline writers have plugged in their laptops to begin laying down boilerplate. It's always safe to open with something like this:

They said the old pro from Providence couldn't take it anymore. They said he had taken too many beatings, too many shots to the head. They said he was old. Tired. Washed up.

All washed up.

All he had left was a heart as big as Federal Hill.

Thump thump. Beating with the will to win. Thump thump. And the pride to carry on.

Thump.

Beating.

If the old pro wins, heart conquers all; if the other guy wins, the hard facts of life KO sentiment again. Either way, the lead works. Soon the sound system will play the ringwalk music for the first bout of the undercard, the first two fighters will make their way through the crowd to the ring, and it will be time for the hitting. Then the writers can finish their stories.

At ringside, you feel yourself to be at the very center of something, but you are actually in a gray borderland between the fights and the world. The action in the raised ring happens far away, even when the clinched fighters are almost on top of you, the ropes bowing outward alarmingly under their weight so that you and the others sitting just below all put up your hands at once, like people getting the spirit at church. But neither are you part of the crowd, exactly. At a major fight, ringside expands to a breadth of fifty feet or more and becomes a populous little district in its own right; the crowd, a largely undifferentiated mass, rises into semidarkness somewhere behind you. The people up there paid for their seats (or were comped by a casino, which means they overpaid for their seats); they expect to be entertained. At least in theory, everybody at ringside has a job to do: staging the fight, governing its conduct, bringing news of it to others.

The distinction can collapse, though. At a local fight, ringside can shrink to a couple of feet wide or less. Once, at the Roxy in downtown Boston, when a union carpenter out of Brockton named Tim "The Hammer" Flamos was fighting Pepe Muniz from Dorchester, an especially enthusiastic supporter of Flamos worked his way forward from his seat down to ringside until he was standing between Charlie Ross and the judge seated to his left, bonking their heads with his elbows as he shouted for Flamos to punch to the body. When Flamos pressed Muniz into the ropes on that side of the ring, the guy reached up with incurved hands and helpfully pointed to the exact places on Muniz's torso he had in mind, his index fingers nearly touching the straining flesh.

This book pursues a ringside course of study at the fights. It follows the progression of humane inquiry, from mystery to learning to mystery again.

Learning at the fights, following the lessons out through the ropes into the wider world beyond boxing, you regularly arrive at the limits of understanding. All sorts of people wrap all sorts of meaning around the fact of meat and bone hitting meat and bone (until one combatant, parted from his senses, becomes nothing more than meat and bone for the duration of a ten-count). The fight world's specialized knowledge supplies the inner layers of that wrapping: lessons in craft, parables of fistic virtue rewarded or un-rewarded, accounts of paydays and rip-offs. Boxing self-consciously takes form around the impulse to discipline hitting, to govern it with rules, to master it with technique and inure the body to its effect. Fight people like to repeat aphorisms, like "Speed is power" or "Styles make fights," that domesticate the wild fact of hitting. They have plenty of extra-fistic company in this undertaking because the res-onance of hitting extends far beyond the fight world's boundaries. Scholars and literary writers and even crusad-ers calling for the abolition of boxing wrap it in more lay-ers: not just the conventions of show business and sport, but also social and artistic and psychological significance. And they keep coming because there's always more work to do. It takes constant effort to keep the slippery, naked, near-formless fact of hitting swaddled in layers of sense and form. Because hitting wants to shake off all encumbering import and just be hitting, because boxing incompletely frames elemental chaos, the capacity of the fights to mean is rivaled by their incapacity to mean anything at all. There is an education in that, too, since education worthy of the name knows its limitations and does not explain things *away.*

The book begins with introductory courses in the first three chapters, which feature initiations into the fights and trace the traffic between formal schooling and a fistic edu-cation. I'm not sure what it says about me and my day job that they also lead in one way or another to college stu-

AT RINGSIDE ■ 15

dents getting whacked in the eye. The middle three chapters, advanced electives, extend the line of inquiry deeper into the fight world and the careers of seasoned campaigners, who, just as much as spectators, struggle to make hitting mean something. The last three chapters, senior seminars, arrive at limits imposed by age, frailty, and the stubborn meaninglessness of hitting. Toward the end of the book, many of the fighters and their counterparts outside the ring are older — wiser, maybe, but also more damaged.

I do not set out to be comprehensive or chronological; I treat boxing as I have found it at ringside and as it persists in memory. The effect of persistence, the way a fight lives in me and I make use of it, tends eventually to silt over the original experience. I bury a fight like a bone and dig it up from time to time to gnaw on it. After a while, I'm tasting mostly my memory of the original meal, but the exercise has contemplative value, and it's good for the teeth. Any sort of bout, not just famous ones, can demand such return visits. Some important fights and fighters appear here, but so do obscure set-tos between journeymen almost nobody has ever heard of. Boxers, whether testing themselves against an opponent or shadowboxing in the mirror, are always reminding me that you can get an education out of whatever you find in front of you, wherever you find it.

1

Halfway

I WAS SITTING on a folding chair at the Larry Holmes Training Center in Easton, Pennsylvania, watching the former champion Holmes, who was forty-six years old and had a fight coming up in eight days, tussle with Linwood Jones in the ring. Jones, a professional sparring partner whose job it was to give the other man a useful workout, was big all over, round-faced, and battened in the midsection with hard fat. Holmes, who in middle age had likewise settled into a build more U- than V-shaped, poked Jones in the face with half-jabs, only occasionally straightening out the punch into its rigorous true form. When he did throw it correctly, Holmes still had a perfect left jab: a crisp straight-arm whipped out from the shoulder with the muscles corded up along its prodigious length and his opponent's head rattling at the end of it. Mostly, though, Holmes worked at protecting himself by trapping the sparring partner's arms, so that the two lurched around the ring stamping and blowing. When Jones got an arm free of Holmes's grip, he threw short hooks to the body, some of which landed, and wide-swinging blows at Holmes's head, which all missed and looked to be thrown mainly for effect. The big swings were protestations of the earnestness with which employee pursued employer, the point being not so much to hit Holmes in the head as to assure him that the punch would have done damage had it landed.

Saoul Mamby, who held the World Boxing Council's super lightweight title from 1980 to 1982 and now served as Holmes's chief second, called out encouragement from his position on the ring apron outside the ropes. He kept up a lilting, cautionary patter — "everything comes from the jab . . . from the jab . . . don't load up, now, don't load up . . . that's right . . . thaaat's right . . . put 'em together . . . now you're having fun" — but Holmes did not appear to be having fun, nor did he appear to heed Mamby's wheedling. He set up in front of the fat man and hit him when and how he wanted to, which was not all the time and not always with sufficient force to mean anything. Everything about the measured, baleful manner of Holmes in the ring said, to cornermen and spectators as well as to his opponent, "I already know how to fight. I've been doing this for a long time. Don't bother me." He went back to his corner between rounds and stood facing Mamby, one gloved hand on the top rope, patiently spitting into a once white bucket and clumsily wiping Vaseline with the other glove onto his face and protective headgear. Holmes was big and dark and old, wearing dark sweatpants and a gray T-shirt soaked through everywhere with his sweat. Mamby, little and light-skinned and more youthful looking than Holmes, with a head of soft, curly hair and a soul patch beneath his lower lip, seemed used to being ignored. He contented himself between rounds with carefully squirting water into Holmes's mouth from a squeeze bottle. He had to rise on tiptoes, reaching over the ropes to shoot all the water into Holmes's mouth.

While I was watching the action an older gentleman sat down next to me. He was closer to Mamby than Holmes in size, closer to Holmes than Mamby in color, and looked to be about seventy — the kind of seventy a person would expect to enjoy after plenty of clean living and regular exercise. "I want you to do me a favor, son," he said. "Will you teach me how to fight?" I smiled and reached to shake the hand he extended. "Earnee Butler," he said. "I figured," I answered, since he couldn't be anybody else. Easton is a town, not a city, and he was the only fistic elder statesman in residence. He launched into a quick autobiographical sketch via a series of questions. Did I know he had fought 104 fights, including one against Jimmy Doyle? That sounded like a lot of fights. Did I know that he had taught Holmes the basics? I had heard something like that. "See that jab?" he said. "I taught him that jab." I said I thought it was a great jab, the best in the heavyweight division for a long time. He made an open-handed "there you have it" gesture and went on: Did I know that he had also worked with Mamby? I did not. Soon he was telling me that fighters always forget who taught them their craft, that fighters are more interested in money than in learning how to fight or honoring their teachers. When they get a little money they stop listening.

"There's things I could still show him," Butler said as Holmes set himself up on the ropes and egged on his next sparring partner, a smaller, trimmer fighter named Art Baylis who rushed in to throw combinations. Baylis, the Pennsylvania cruiserweight champion, moved in and out looking for openings and punched with more conviction than Jones. Holmes rolled grimacing on the ropes and blocked punches, cuffing Baylis with his left and occasionally dropping his right hand to thump him under the heart. "But I stay out," Butler continued. "You can't tell them anything. See that other fellow, the short one in the corner? I taught him too. That's Sal Mamby." Butler leaned close and prodded my elbow when he talked; there was a musty but not unpleasant smell about him, like that of a house filled with broken-in, lived-with things. His eyes were large and wet. For a man who fought professionally for years, he did not have a lot of scar tissue in his face. I thought that he must have had a good jab, too, the kind that scuttles opponents' balance and timing, preventing them from landing hard punches.

We watched the sparring peacefully. Butler leaned over now and again to tell me things: that his mother had been careful not to let him know how proud she was after his

first fight; that the purpose of learning to fight was self-
defense rather than hurting others; that he had taught
Holmes and Mamby; that his wife, a good judge of character, had told him to watch out for Don King (who wooed
Holmes away from Butler with promises of big money). He
produced a business card and gave it to me. "Do you have
any children?" he asked. Not yet. "Okay," he said, "because if you had a son I would teach him how to fight." I
asked about the various kids and young men going through
their paces in the gym. "I help them, most of them," he
said. "That's mostly what I do. But I tell them, you got to
work hard and you got to listen. If they don't pay attention,
I don't bother. See that fella in the corner there. That's Sal
Mamby. I taught *him*."

Holmes, having finished eight rounds of sparring, leaned
forward into his corner with both forearms across the
top rope and his head down. Shoving Jones around and
weathering the assaults of Baylis had worn him out, and he
was breathing heavily without bothering to conceal it. He
looked as if he had showered with his clothes on. His seconds struggled to take off his headgear, gloves, and foul
protector. Freed of the gear, Holmes began shadowboxing
in the ring to warm down, but he went back to his corner
massaging his side and burping with difficulty. He said
something I didn't catch to Mamby, who stepped lightly
away from the corner, saying, "If it will make you feel
better . . ." Holmes hooked the bucket with one foot and
positioned it in front of him, then stood over it with his
back to the room. Straightening up and turning slightly to

the right, with his left hand on the ropes and his right hand to his mouth, he struck a pose like Tarzan when he gave his signature call in the movies. After a moment Holmes brought his hand away from his mouth, looked down, and vomited a reddish watery cascade into the bucket. Holmes is tall, and the vomit fell far enough to make a sharp report when it hit the bucket's insides. He went back to his Tarzan position and repeated the operation six or seven times. He showed no signs of distress, standing straight and not spasming at all. He made no noise other than a low gasp between the last two repetitions. Each successive shower was clearer, more watery and less solid. At some point in the process Mamby said as if making conversation, "You ate late today," and Holmes nodded before putting hand to mouth again. Holmes's small crew of seconds and advisers stood around respectfully, waiting for him to finish. They, and the handful of spectators who had wandered in to watch him train, approved of this performance. If one eats too late, we all silently agreed, this seems to be the correct way to handle the problem. We nodded and half smiled at one another, pleased in a right-tool-for-the-right-job way. When he was done, and the bucket sat in a vile pool of near misses, Holmes went back to warming down and Mamby went for a mop.

The purging improved Holmes's mood. He washed his mouth out with the squeeze bottle and returned to training with new vigor, climbing down out of the ring to get on the StairMaster and charging at it while joking with his seconds and singing occasional nonsense syllables. The rest of the fighters in the gym felt the change in climate and went lustily at their own work.

One of them was Russell, a pale, dedicated-looking young man of modest size and shape. He had hit the heavy bag early, before Holmes got into the ring, then jumped rope facing the ring (rather than the mirrors lining the gym's back wall) so he could watch the master spar. Now finished for the day, changed into jeans and a sweatshirt and toting his gym bag, Russell hung around to talk with the various sages in Holmes's crew as they waited for the boss to finish on the StairMaster. From my seat across the room I watched him huddled with a thick, serene guy named Cliff. Putting down his bag, Russell broke away to sketch a sparring problem: "See? See," he seemed to say as he stomped back and forth and threw for-example punches, "it's a problem." Cliff offered a solution with understated movements that filled the gaps left by Russell's: you just take a small step here, and turn your shoulder like so, and you don't have a problem anymore.

I knew Russell slightly because he was a student at Lafayette College, where I taught. He ran in Easton's cemetery every other morning, and weekday afternoons he walked the mile and a half down from College Hill across town to the gym — and back again, uphill, unless someone gave him a ride home. "Besides schoolwork, this is about all I do," he once told me. A few weeks before, I had watched him spar in the ring after Holmes was done for the day. Russell moved forward, throwing the fundamental one-two combination — left jab, right cross — on which

Holmes built his fortune, while Angel, a short high school kid preparing for an upcoming amateur fight, leaped in and out to deliver flurries of hooks and overarm rights. Russell was bigger and stronger than Angel and, throwing straight punches inside the arc of Angel's wilder swings, should have given him a pounding. But Russell's footwork could not get him in close enough. He had to lunge forward with his upper body and arms, rather than driving with his legs, to make contact with his opponent. Consequently, his punches lacked snap and he tended to be off balance. He pursued Angel diligently, and hit him a few times, but took too many punches in return. At the end of the day, with a welt on his nose and angry red marks on his face despite the headgear, Russell had seemed disappointed in his showing but undiscouraged. He had gained some experience, perhaps he had learned something about spacing, and the lesson had not cost him too dearly. "It's a good thing he couldn't hit that hard, at least," he told me later. "Some guys hit so hard you have a real problem."

This time, Russell was going home unmarked. When I gave him a ride up the hill I asked why he wasn't sparring these days. "I thought I better go back to basics," he said. I agreed that was a good idea. The unspoken addendum "because it looked like you were going to get your head bashed in" hung in the air between us for a moment and evaporated. He fell to talking about the appeal of boxing. "It's helped me a lot," he said, "even in my personal life. You know, the fact that it's painful, that there's pain, makes you have to be disciplined. You have to work, stay with it."

Maybe because I was a professor, he mentioned Ernest Hemingway, Joyce Carol Oates, and the sense of history that permeates the air of a boxing gym. I think he was humoring me. (I don't mind being humored if it's done with good intentions, so I told him about two recent versions of the *Iliad* in which the boxer Epeus speaks to the Achaean army in Muhammad Ali's distinctive voice — "I am the greatest" — thereby reversing the conventional flow of literary influence from past to present.) When we got back to the groomed precincts of College Hill, the hard-boiled town having fallen away behind us, I pulled the car over to let him out. I said "Good luck," and meant it. He was game, curious, and sincere enough to get himself hurt. I hoped that his mentors at the gym would help him teach himself what he needed to know before that happened.

Holmes won the fight he was training for, and the next one, then retired. Then he unretired and fought some more. He had been promising to quit and then breaking those promises for more than a decade, but the balance of risk to gain would tip, finally, past the point where another fight would be worth his while.

Holmes has always seemed to draw strength from a heightened sense of scarcity and grievance. There is only so much money in the world, only so much respect; there are only so many championships, even in this age of multiple sanctioning bodies and titles. He has treated the task of winning in the ring as a zero-sum process of taking his share away from other people. It has been, as he sees it, a

solitary struggle against enemies in the ring and everywhere outside it: boxing people who have withheld the recognition he deserved, promoters who have robbed him,
people in town who resent his fortune. For more than three
decades, Holmes has been going to the gym to get his own,
to harden his body and sharpen his skills for the war of
each against all. Between family life, minding his investments (which is what he does all day when he isn't training), and negotiating the boxer's routines — sleeping and
eating right, running, getting loose, keeping his footwork
precise, blocking punches, recognizing openings in his opponent's style and hitting into them, matching the form of
each movement to its purpose — he has not had much left
over for the other fighters in the gym.

But in recent years he has begun talking about passing on
to young fighters the reserve of technical skill and ring experience he has accumulated. He took a particular interest
in Angel, who had been winning amateur fights. Holmes
said he wanted to teach him how to jab, how to break a
jaw. That kind of concentrated, patient attention to a student would entail a major change in the way Holmes in-
habits the gym. Single-minded and surly when he trains for
fights, Holmes has not devoted more than throwaway energy to the young apprentices around him. Once in a while
he encourages somebody to work harder or yells at somebody to stop fucking around. One day I saw him interrupt
his warm-down to bellow "Bad habits, bad habits gonna
cause you problems" at a twelve-year-old girl with a blond
ponytail who was jumping rope in front of the wall of mir-

rors. He spent a minute showing her the right way to do it. The skinny girl watched carefully, nodding, while the big sweaty grandfather jumped, light and quick and in lovely balance, whipping the rope back and forth and side to side, saying, "Like this . . . see?" They both had their hands wrapped.

If Holmes has not devoted himself actively to instruction, he has been on display, and those with initiative could teach themselves by observing him. For people like Baylis, Angel, Russell, and the little blond girl, who have been going to the Larry Holmes Training Center to train alongside or against a former champion, the model of learning has been a master's studio. The lesser practitioners and apprentices school themselves by observing Holmes go about his business at the end of a very long, accomplished career. He has given them his example and access (for a modest monthly fee, which he has been known to waive) to the gym, where they could find lessons and teachers like Earnee Butler and Holmes's cornermen. To learn from Holmes, other fighters have had to meet him more than halfway, by devoting themselves to boxing and by working from his example. Russell was in this sense a model student. His daily journey down the hill from college was in some ways the longest made by any of the gym's regulars.

When I lived in Easton, I used to go down to the gym regularly in the afternoons, not only to watch Holmes train but also to put distance between myself and campus. I went there to get away from some things and to go toward others. I got away from college; from a world dominated by students who don't always come halfway to their teachers, and by professors in the habit of coming more than halfway to make up the difference. I went toward the feeling of being in Easton, and not on College Hill looking down at it; toward the insular profession of pugilism an ocean away from the subcontinent of the academy. I got away from being a teacher; from the constant setting up of oneself as telling, helping, asking, modeling, evaluating; from the duty of showing people why and how they should care (at least for fifteen weeks) about what I care about; from a classroom in which I must depend on everyone else's initiative and perseverance to accomplish anything. I went toward writing: I was at the gym to gather material, I could tell myself, from which I would build an essay, maybe a book, the published prose that writers in the academy call "my work." Having come down the hill after teaching class, I took special pleasure in the self-interest of finding what I could and using it without sharing the project with collaborators, and without considering responsibility — except to the material, and perhaps to a reader someday.

Of course I was running in a circle, because what I saw at the Larry Holmes Training Center was teaching and learning: things done wrong and corrected (or done wrong repeatedly, and suffered from accordingly); things done right over and over until they are habits that shape lives; knowledge with consequences. And, of course, everybody in the gym — especially an observer like me — depends on the others in order to accomplish anything. Even Holmes, the master, needed his sparring partners: Linwood Jones, who leaned intimately on his boss, shouting, "Hit me! That all you got? Hit me! Yaaah!"; Art Baylis, who surged in to test the palisade of Holmes's elbows and fists. Without them, Holmes could not prepare his body and technique for the next fight. When he was a young man aspiring to greatness, Holmes worked as a sparring partner for Muhammad Ali, Joe Frazier, and Earnie Shavers, soaking up all the ring craft he could from the best fighters around. As an old fighter sparring with younger men, Holmes had to teach himself all over again, every day, in front of everybody else in the gym, to fight like Larry Holmes. Every serious fighter in the gym is teacher and student, is in fact his or her own most dedicated pupil.

When he gave me his card, Earnee Butler said, "That's yours. Read it — both sides." He said it as if reading both sides were a particular procedure, known to insiders, with which to get the most out of the equipment. On one side was printed:

If you can take discipline and hard knocks
Earnee Butler will teach you how to box
Earnee Butler
Maker of Champions

Home	Gym
258-3042	253-8271

On the other side:

If We meet and you forget me,
you have lost nothing;

> but if you meet JESUS CHRIST
> and forget Him, then you
> have lost everything.

It got me thinking what the two messages on the card, both framed with the contingent "If," might have to do with each other. The front of the card is about taking care of yourself: sharpening and strengthening yourself through disciplined application, learning to protect yourself by doing things regularly and the right way. A teacher, or an opponent, can help you with that. The back, even for those of us with no special commitment to Jesus, is about the opposite impulse: opening yourself to others and to what they know, cultivating the generosity and receptiveness of spirit that grow from moral confidence. Students can help you with that. Teachers, like students, learn to balance the two impulses, which is something I try to bear in mind as I go up the hill and down the hill: do enough of what's on the front of the card to enable yourself to think as the back of the card asks you to.

2

Cut Time

Russell came up at the end of class one day to tell me
there would be a card of fights held in a couple of weeks in
nearby Allentown. He knew I was interested in boxing and
thought I might like to go; also, he needed a ride. I had figured he was not stopping by to continue our discussion of
"Bartleby the Scrivener." Seated front and center, in a posture of polite interest but not taking many notes, Russell
followed the action in class without committing to it. Some
students, infighters, sit up front to get your attention, but
others do it for the opposite reason: one way to avoid getting hit is to get in too close to your opponent, nestling co-
zily against his clavicle, where he can't apply the leverage to
hurt you (unless he fouls by headbutting, biting ears, or
calling on people who don't raise their hands). Russell did

the reading and wrote his papers, but he was not swept up by fictions and make-believe characters. The class met in the afternoon just before he headed down the hill to the gym and I suspected that he was thinking about the imminent shock of punching rather than the literary matters at hand.

Every once in a while, though, Russell would say something that showed me he was paying attention. Impressed by Frederick Douglass's late-round TKO of the overseer Covey, he spoke up to remind us that this scene dramatized the red-blooded ideal of self-making with one's own two hands. But he had also been moved to speak by Melville's Bartleby, who comprehensively rejects one of the fight world's foundational principles: protect yourself at all times. Russell, breaking form, had his hand up first and initiated the discussion of Bartleby with references to Gandhi, Martin Luther King, and the difficult stance of moral inaction. Russell encouraged us to consider whether the pacific Bartleby, by preferring to do nothing, was making a gesture in protest of his situation or was simply not much good with his hands and therefore destined to be acted upon by a world that kept the hard knocks coming in a steady stream. At least that's what I took him to mean, and I got busy parlaying it into a general discussion in which Russell, having said his piece, declined to participate further.

Once the other students had risen to the bait and were doing the talking, I had a chance to look Russell over for new damage. This week it was a thick, dark line, like lavishly applied lampblack, that ran under his right eye from nose to cheekbone. Another black eye, and this one a prize-winner. One of the quiet dramas of having Russell in class was seeing what kind of punishment he had incurred of late. He was so placid in manner, so Bartleby-like in his pale decency, that the various lumps, welts, and bruises passing over his face like weather fronts always jarred me. Having seen him spar in the gym, I shouldn't have been surprised. He was strong but not quick, and he came straight at his antagonist, equably accepting blows as the price of getting into range to deliver the one-twos he favored. I knew that Russell's style ensured he would get hit often, even on his best days, but when I saw the marks of his latest lesson a little click of alarmed recognition still ran through me as I managed the discussion and scrawled on the blackboard, chalk dust all over my hands and on the thighs of my pants where I wiped them.

I gestured at the new black eye when Russell stopped after class to tell me about the upcoming fight card. He just said "Sterling," looked at the floor, and shook his head, smiling faintly. Sterling was one of the gym's rising stars, a teenager already poised and smooth in the ring. Russell had several years and a few pounds on him, although neither advantage did Russell much good. Sterling had fallen half in love with his own preternatural speed and cleverness, with the idea of his own genius. That, and a tendency to switch back and forth too promiscuously between right- and left-handed stances in order to baffle his opponents, was his only evident weakness. He was the kind of evasive, willowy counterpuncher that solid hitters long to pummel.

Russell, for one, believed with doctrinaire intensity that he could hurt Sterling if only he could catch him. I had not seen the two of them spar together, but I had seen Russell's face after their sessions and I had seen both of them spar with others, so I could imagine the encounters: Russell following Sterling doggedly around the ring, absorbing jabs and the occasional speed-blurred combination as he sought to fix the skinny body and weaving head in his sights long enough to throw a meaningful punch. When Russell's thoughts drifted far away during class, I assumed he was stalking Sterling in his mind's eye, hoping finally to nail him with a big right hand.

On our drive down to the fights later that month, Russell said he was disappointed in his progress as a boxer. He had been scheduled to make his first amateur fight in the Golden Gloves, but he had canceled it. He knew he wasn't ready. I asked if Sterling was still beating him up in the sparring ring, and he said, "Well, yeah, him, but also everybody else. A while ago I was walking around with two black eyes and loose cartilage in my nose and I started to get . . . *discouraged* thinking about it." Russell wanted to win an official boxing match, not just to spar or fight creditably, but the accumulating pain and damage made him worry that he might be foolish to pursue this goal any further. At the same time, he was wary of giving up too easily, of mistaking for perpetual futility what might only be a difficult period in his fistic education. He said, "When I spar I'm getting really beat up, like, humiliated, in there. I can't get better until I practice more, but I can't practice without getting beat up." I asked why he couldn't stop now, with no significant damage done, having learned the basics of boxing and something about disciplined hard work, and having gotten a dose of the kind of violent extremity from which college usually shelters people like him and me.

Russell had two answers to that. First, the ever-present threat of hurt and humiliation in boxing inspired him to rigor in his training, and he worried that if he stopped going to the gym he would backslide in other endeavors requiring discipline as well. "When I first got to college," he said, "I slacked off a lot, just hung out and messed around, and it really affected me — my school work, my life. But once I found boxing, I got disciplined about everything. School, eating, sleeping, everything. This week I was getting really discouraged and I didn't go down to the gym at all, and I already felt myself letting things go. You know, falling back into bad habits." Second, he said, discipline aside, "It could turn out that pain and damage are important just by themselves. That's a kind of life experience you can't get as a middle-class college student. Maybe it's worth getting banged up to learn about yourself and, you know, the rest of the world." There were guys down at the gym who had been in jail, who had been addicted to drugs, who had given and taken beatings in and out of the ring, who had been out on the streets broke and without prospects. That was what Russell meant by "life experience."

He seemed to want an argument, so I gave him one. Boxing was certainly not the only way to sample the world beyond College Hill. Most experience of that world fell somewhere between the extremes of reading about it in books and insisting on getting punched out over and over by experts. Warming to the task, I argued that his fixation on getting hurt as the key to authentic "life experience" took the school out of the school of hard knocks, reducing an education in pugilism to an elaborate form of self-abuse. If ritual humiliation and physical damage became his antidote to slacking off and a sheltered upbringing, how could that formula for gaining "life experience" give him good reason to improve as a boxer? And, anyway, what made boxing necessarily a better path to "life experience" than college? Wasn't college, ideally, supposed to be about exactly the things he saw in boxing: rigorous self-knowledge, encounters with the wider world, and the inculcation of virtues like discipline? After all, Frederick Douglass presents himself as a student first and a wordsmith last — a reader, writer, and speaker. In his autobiography he disdains boxing, like whiskey-drinking, as a waste of a Sabbath day better spent learning to read, and he fights only twice — when cornered, rather than going in search of beatings — in a definitively unsheltered life.

Russell said "I see that" and "Right, right" in the way a person does when he has stated his position; he is pleased that you agree it's worth discussing, and nothing you say can change it.

We were on our way to see Art Baylis fight on the evening's card. Art was getting old in fighter-years. Sometimes, wrapping his hands before he got to work at Larry Holmes's gym, he would complain, "I'm tired of this bullshit. I'm not making money, I'm getting all beat up for nothing." The other fighters were sympathetic. It's a rough business, they would agree, nobody here is getting rich. (Actually, Holmes had been rich for some time, but that was different.) Some tried to jolly Art out of his dark moods, but he would say, "Don't *tell* me I'm not tired," and they let him be, exchanging smiles behind his back. They knew he would be back the next day, or the day after that. Art fought for small purses and worked as a sparring partner. When he sparred he sometimes wore not just the standard headgear but a mask, a simultaneously futuristic- and medieval-looking helmet made of bright red cushiony material mounted on a rigid frame that fit over his whole head. It had two slits at the eyes and projected out, beaklike, over his nose, mouth, and jaw. He had been cut up over the years and there was no reason to open old wounds in the gym.

Art had turned pro relatively late, in his mid-twenties, and there were gaps in his record, periods of almost two years and four and a half years in which he had not fought at all. There was talk of a stretch in the joint and a drug problem that had undercut his development as a fighter. A small, competent heavyweight who also fought as a cruiserweight, he was still solid in the legs, but his chest drooped. Shirtless, he did not look like God in a painting. Sports fans who worship armor-plate pectorals and speak of "intimidation" and "crunch time" might make the mistake of thinking Art was soft and could be overwhelmed by a younger man in better shape. Art knew better. He did best fighting anatomically impressive whippersnappers who invested more in their bodies than in their craft, men who had the advantage of him *only* in youth and physique.

Art was not necessarily quicker or more gifted than the men he beat. Rather, he knew how to fight and had few expectations of glorious success to interfere with his capacity to endure hard going. He had won enough fights to know what it felt like to outlast the other man, but he had been beaten up often enough to know what a well-crafted beating should feel like. He knew the difference between that and a couple of rounds of rough treatment at the hands of an opponent who will soon have overextended himself in the flush of incipient triumph. Typically, Art lost or split the early rounds, throwing his left jab and hook to the head, holding his right hand in reserve, and weathering the other guy's best shots. After a couple of rounds of this, once both men had spent the first increments of energy and were taking stock of what remained, just about the time when a younger man begins to realize with some distress that he is tired and there's still a day's work to do, Art settled in to win the fight: he began pounding the body with both hands to slow his opponent down and discourage further offense, then went back upstairs to the head.

On the night Russell and I went to see him fight in the ballroom of the Days Inn in Allentown, Art got cut badly in the second round of a bout scheduled for ten. The other fighter, Exum Speight, was a professional opponent, considerably younger than Art but with more fights and many more losses on his record. The matchmaker had chosen

Speight with the expectation that Art would defeat him, perhaps after a crowd-pleasing struggle. Although Speight rarely won a bout anymore, he had gone the distance with many of the best in the business and he looked the part of a tough guy. While Art's size and strength resided in his thick legs, Speight's resided in his upper body: bulky shoulders, prominent veins branching across biceps and forearms, a strongbox of a chest. Speight came out briskly, circling and firing punches in a commanding rhythm. Art followed him around the ring, eating jabs and throwing left jabs and hooks of his own, looking for an opening to deliver the right. Perhaps because Speight was acting as if he expected to win, and seemed unaffected by the older man's punches, Art forgot himself. He became impatient and tried his right hand too early, before the younger man's force had been sufficiently denatured by frustration, fatigue, and punishment. Art loaded up leverage to throw a right at the head through what looked like a gap in his opponent's defense, but Speight sensed Art's balance shifting. He snapped his left hand up and around to deliver a crisp hook that interrupted Art's own slower-developing punch and landed flush to the right side of Art's face. There was soft, much-torn old scar tissue around the outside corner of Art's right eye, the kind that parts like wet paper when force is applied to it. Blood came up enthusiastically out of the mess, a rich, awful, seductive red under the ring lights. Within seconds it was running down Art's face, getting all over his chest and Speight's gloves, then Art's own gloves and both fighters' trunks. Art's white trunks began to turn pink.

When blood from a serious cut finds its way into the lights, everything seems to change: it's cut time. You can almost hear it, a droning almost-music that hangs in the smoke-filled air of fight night, strumming the optic nerves and vibrating in the teeth, encouraging fighters to do urgent, sometimes desperate things. Spectators, too, shamed and fascinated, plunge headlong into cut time. What was inside and hidden, implicit in the fight, has come outside and taken form.

Art grabbed Speight as often as he could and held him, hoping to make it through the rest of the second round without further damage. To shield the wound, Art put the uncut left side of his face against the left side of Speight's in the clinches, which created the illusion that Art was searching the crowd for someone over Speight's shoulder. Unhinged by cut time, I imagined for one bizarre moment that he was trying to make eye contact with me (at ringside) and Russell (back in the crowd somewhere) in order to call on us. "See? 'Life experience.' Discuss." A great slick of fresh blood covered the right side of Art's face, which was stretched into a desperate-looking grimace. It was hard not to believe he was silently entreating us, the referee — anybody — to stop the fight. But of course he was doing no such thing. Art had an education, not only in fighting but in being hurt, that made the cut a problem to solve. He had to negotiate the difficulties of cut time while conducting the fight back into more manageable form. He had sprung a leak and he needed to fix it.

Art bled and bled. The ring doctor visited his corner between rounds to inspect the damage. Art's seconds, seasoned practitioners who had worked more illustrious corners in the past, stanched the flow as best they could, but the cut opened anew as soon as Speight started hitting it in the next round. Art knew he was in danger and picked up the pace, throwing wilder punches in the hope of hurting his man before the cut obliged the ring doctor to stop the fight. Driven out of his customarily measured boxing style, Art began to make a sobbing, effortful noise as he threw outsize blows. Most of them missed, which caused him to sob more dramatically as he expended even more energy to regain his balance after every staggering miss. But some of his blows hit Speight's guard or landed glancingly to the chin or body. Speight, instead of counterpunching in earnest to make Art pay for exposing himself so rashly, changed tactics and waited for the older man to run out of steam. Speight made a fort out of his forearms and gloves, risking only an occasional sortie to throw a punch in the lulls between Art's assaults. This went on for another three rounds. Art's blood splattered both fighters, the canvas underfoot, and the judges, functionaries, and reporters at ringside. A slick-haired guy from the boxing commission, seated a few places down from me at the long table abutting the ring apron, pulled up the white tablecloth and tented it over himself to the eyes. Perhaps he was squeamish, or protecting his suit, or worried about AIDS. The referee was awash in the blood, but did not seem to mind; he had been bled on before.

(Later, at the end of the night, the referee used a stopped-up sink in the men's room to soak his shirt. A beefy fellow with an iron-gray crewcut and copious body hair, he had stripped down to a dark blue sleeveless T-shirt and was kneading his once light blue dress shirt in the pool of pink water. He had taken off his black bow tie and once white surgical gloves and set them at the edge of the sink. One of the gloves, inside out, seemed to be pointing a finger at the mess in the sink. It looked as if he had performed a successful roadside appendectomy with his car tools on the way home from an evening at the Rotary Club. Men from the audience made wide detours around him on their way to the urinals, all except one of which had backed up and were no longer flushing. The referee patiently did his laundry amid the comings and goings of men, the cigarette smoke, the cloying stink of deodorant cakes in the urinals, and the strong, astringent smell of beer drinkers' piss.)

It took a couple of rounds for the spectators, who flinched every time flying blood caught the lights, to realize that Art was winning the fight. His punching frenzy gradually wore Speight down, accomplishing the goal Art typically pursued with several more rounds' worth of studied sharpshooting. Speight appeared to be in good shape, but having a groaning, bloodied maniac flailing after him for long three-minute stretches seemed to drain his energy and resolve. By the fifth round he was no longer circling, no longer throwing many punches. He snapped occasional jabs at Art, but none of them landed near the cut and they didn't bother Art much. Art, realizing he had messily completed an important task — breaking Speight's initial energy and confidence — and was now ahead of schedule to win by decision, reined himself in but kept up the pressure. He began to land hard, accurate punches and Speight found himself backing sulkily toward the ropes, well behind on points, as usual. Having taken command of the fight, Art threw rights with renewed authority, confident that Speight would not take advantage of the openings for counterpunching that he created. The younger man's offense slacked off to almost nothing. By midfight, Art was no longer bleeding from the cut next to his right eye, and only a little from another cut in the scar tissue on the bridge of his nose; Speight, though, bled in a slow, dark flow from both nostrils.

Cut time was over. Its droning, atonal almost-music modulated into a straight-ahead 4/4 standard: The Exum Speight Loses Another Fight Blues.

Both men tired, and both had gone the distance often enough to be familiar with bone-deep exhaustion, but Art was better at fighting to win in that state. He seemed to welcome fatigue as a condition in his favor, in the way that certain racehorses favor a muddy track. For Speight, being tired was part of a familiar process in which resolve gave way to resignation and, almost inevitably, to the referee's raising the other man's taped hand. Experience had formed a rut rather than a reserve in him. One problem with being tough and strong is that the realization of being bested, of feeling the other fighter's hands shaping the bout, comes as a dispiriting shock every time, no matter how often it happens and no matter how familiar it becomes. Speight, having become excited and perhaps even a bit frightened when he saw that Art was badly cut, and having plunged into a depression when Art had not quit because of the cut, now looked as if he had a headache and wanted to go home. But Art — tired as he was and would be, without grandiose prospects but possessed of a thick and instructive past — had found his rhythm. He moved fluidly and with energetic purpose, cutting off the ring, controlling Speight's movements with jabs and double jabs, snapping Speight's head back with jarring rights. Speight roused himself to hit Art on the chin, a hard shot, after the bell at the end of the fifth round; Art, unshaken, grinned evilly at him before going back to his corner. Both of them knew that Speight already regarded the fight as lost and done with. If a professional opponent in good fighting trim has gone deep enough into a bout to be genuinely tired, it means he has already earned his paycheck by putting up a creditable battle.

Storybook logic does not apply to tank-town fights. Once Art had the fight in hand, there was no reason for him to get all crazy in trying to knock Speight out. As Art piled up rounds with the judges, he became more careful. By the end he was doing just enough to win every round, and the two men spent the last couple of rounds leaning on each other, for which Speight had a point deducted by the blood-soaked referee. Art won the decision by a wide margin on every judge's card. It had been a difficult job of work, and he had been obliged to do it the hard way, as usual.

Russell did not talk much on the ride back to Easton later that night; we sped along the highway in reflective silence. When I got home, having dropped him off along the curving drive that bisected the darkened campus, my wife was sleeping and the house was still. Fight night was in my head, strong against the stillness, as I made my way through the dark house and up the stairs: the red gloves and infinitely redder blood, the moving bodies, the ceaseless oceanic sound made by even a small fight crowd, the clarity of every stain and thread under the ring lights, the smoke, the shock of solid punches, the complicated rhythms of clinches and infighting, the high, wavering almost-note òf cut time. Bending in front of the bathroom sink to wash my face, I looked in the mirror and discovered that there were bright spots of blood on my pale green shirt. Three more, crusted and almost black, made a kind of Orion's Belt across my forehead. I had already noticed at ringside that there was blood on my notes and my pants. It was almost certainly all Art's, although I suppose some of it could have come from Speight's nose. I washed my face and then I ran water in the sink to soak the shirt.

In the months that followed, Russell found a teacher, a retired fighter who sometimes worked with novices, and eventually declared himself ready to try the Golden Gloves. He was wrong. He described his amateur debut as an out-of-body nightmare. He felt himself submerged in a flat-footed torpor in which he moved with desperately inappropriate serenity while the other fighter, unspeakably quick and confident, pounded him at will. Russell was not badly hurt, but he was thoroughly beaten. After the first round, the referee came to his corner to ask if he wished to continue; he did, but the referee stopped the bout in the second. Feeling himself profoundly out of place in the ring and in his own body, sustained only by courage once his craft had deserted him, seemingly unable to defend himself or fight back, Russell had frozen, as novices sometimes do. "I never got started," he told me. "It was like I wasn't even there."

I moved away from Easton soon after, but, back to visit a year later, I dropped by the Larry Holmes Training Center one afternoon. The fighters poured sweat in the late September heat. Stripped to a black tank top and shorts, Art was hitting a heavy bag steadily and well — first the left hand twice, a jab and a hook, then a right cross. Somebody was hitting the other heavy bag very hard; it jumped with each blow, and the thump-crack of sharp punching filled the long, low room. When the second hitter moved around his bag and out from behind Art, I could see it was Russell. There was a new weight and speed in his punching, and he had his legs and shoulders into the making of each punch. His diligence and his teacher's efforts had evidently paid off in an improved command of leverage. He was working on power shots: his left hooks made a perfect L from shoulder to glove, staving in the bag on one side; his straight rights imparted the illusion of animate sensitivity to the bag as it leaped away from the impact. He looked bigger than before, having begun to fill out, but more than that, he looked looser, more competent, more alert. He had lost the undersea quality of abstraction that had always surrounded him in the gym. There was confident vigor in the way he shoved the bag away so it would swing back at him. He looked forward to its arrival because he was going to hit it just right, with all of himself behind the gloved fist.

I raised an eyebrow at Jeff, a stocky gym regular who worked for the grounds crew up at the college in the mornings and for Holmes in the afternoons. He looked over at Russell, smiled and nodded, then said, "Yeah, Russ has been getting it together. He can *hit*, man. He was in sparring with one of those boys last week and the guy's head was just going like this: bop! bop! bop!" With each bop! he threw his head back, chin up, like a fighter getting tagged. One of Holmes's seconds, a round, characteristically abrupt fellow named Charlie, chimed in: "Russ can hit. No doubt about it. He had his problems for a while, he got beat up, but he stayed with it and he's getting good. He gets in there this time, he'll surprise some people. Hurt 'em." This was wildly enthusiastic praise coming from Charlie, who usually ignored the younger fighters in the gym except to shoo them out of the ring when Holmes was ready to work out.

Loyal to one of the gym's most diligent apprentices, if not one of its most talented, Jeff and Charlie were talking Russell up to one of his professors, but anyone could see he had made an important step forward on the way from dabbler to fighter. It looked as if he had arrived at a sense of belonging in the gym, not because he was training next to Art, but because he was doing it right and knew himself to be doing it right. The Golden Gloves beating had helped to drive home the lesson that just wanting to be in the ring is not a good enough reason to be there; you have to accept responsibility for your part in the mutual laying on of hands. I expected that Russell would not freeze up in his next fight. He was still slow and hittable, and he might well lose, but if so he would lose not because he felt out of place in the ring but because he was outboxed or made mistakes or was simply not quick enough. And if the other guy let Russell get started throwing punches, Russell might just give him a beating, or at least a stiff punch or two to remember him by.

When I got back home to Boston I wrote Russell an e-mail saying I was pleased to see that he had made such progress in the gym. I admitted I had worried in the past that he would get seriously hurt, perhaps even in a life-changing way, because he was in the gym for the wrong reasons — to absorb "life experience" passively rather than to train actively at a craft — but I was less worried now that he had evidently gotten down to work in earnest. I was surprised, then, when Russell wrote back a couple of weeks later to announce a retirement of sorts:

> In earnest, I have become somewhat disenchanted with boxing. There seems to be a level, which I have reached, at which it has lost to some extent its seductive and mesmorizing effect. While I will always retain an interest and awe in the sport, I feel that I can understand the subtleties of the sport and could even execute them given the proper conditioning and practice. While I regard Larry and other successfull boxers with the utmost respect and admiration, there seems to be a lack of transcendence into a higher state of more complete perfection in the human realm.

Financial gain does not take the fighter out of the street and its culture, nor does it provide him with any solice or real advancement. I may be sounding somewhat highbrow, however, I now realize that I have bigger fish to fry. With my college education quickly coming to a close I need to focus the resource of my time on things which will propell my advancement after graduation. I will certainly remain active in training and boxing but I realistically can no longer give it my full commitment (and just when I was starting to see the fruit of my labor) . . .

Still in need of an appropriate nickname,

Russell

Seduction, proper conditioning and practice, a lack of transcendence, bigger fish to fry, a reapportioning of resources: a college man's romance with boxing in brief.

Russell's retirement should not have surprised me. He finished with boxing when he had learned enough — about hitting and about being hit, about other people and himself, about what Douglass and Bartleby had to say about "life experience" — to understand how fighters submit to being molded by one another. The long line of men who had hit Art in the right eye had contributed to making him a man who could handle cut time. If the line got longer, though, Art would inevitably deform his style to protect the weak spot, leaving new openings for opponents to exploit. Too much of that would cause Art to end up like Exum Speight. The already too long line of men who had outpunched Speight had taught him to expect defeat and even collaborate in it. Red-blooded convention treats boxing as a matter of one fighter asserting himself forcefully over another, but boxing is just as much a matter of accepting that what you become rests in the hands of others. Or in the hands of orchestrated circumstance: summoned to Allentown to lose a fight, Speight did not set out to initiate cut time in the second round of his bout with Art; he just counterpunched into a hole in the hometown favorite's defense. Had Russell gone further than he did in boxing — and especially had he turned pro, shedding the amateur's protective headgear — he would have had to accept cut time as a reasonable possibility, a condition likely to be thrust upon a hard hitter who takes too many punches in return. Both Art and Speight, the man who was cut and the man who cut him, knew themselves to *deserve* cut time. Russell quit before reaching that stage of resignation (and before he felt he deserved a ring name — like, say, Russell the Destroyer, or Russell the Scrivener), but he went far enough that his Golden Gloves opponent, his trainer, and his sparring partners helped him get the feel and the sense of a boxer's resignation in his body, where they will persist.

Russell carried six courses in his last semester of college, which left little time for boxing. He said, "I'll spar again, maybe, but I don't think I will fight in the Golden Gloves. I'm too busy, and I'm not as hungry as I was. It's not worth the risk." Art, of course, kept fighting. I've seen him in action twice since then. In the first bout, he suffered a dubious first-round knockout at the hands of a prospect named Baby Joe Mesi. The first time Mesi threw a hard punch, Art went over backward and lay still, like a Hollywood stuntman leveled by an action hero. It was a record-padder for Mesi, a quick if humiliating payday for Art. In the second bout, a difficult victory of the kind in which Art specializes, he outlasted an opponent from Philadelphia named Byron Jones. The victory evened Art's lifetime record at thirteen wins and thirteen losses. After sixteen years of hard going in and out of the ring, he had fought the business to a bloody draw.

3

Mismatches

Most fights are mismatches. The bigger and stronger shove around the smaller and weaker; those who know how to fight go after those who don't; the sibling who always wins picks on the one who always loses. Same goes for nations; animals, too. Mismatches are natural enough. Nobody cries foul when a whip-fast snake eats a nice plump mouse.

Let us define a mismatch as a contest in which fundamental differences in ability dictate that only one side has a reasonable chance to win. Not every one-sided contest is a mismatch, though. It may happen, for example, that Notre Dame's football team plays extraordinarily well one afternoon and crushes Michigan in a one-sided game, but that result doesn't make the game a mismatch. The schools have made comparable investments in the sport, they have played against similar competition, each has defeated the other in recent memory, and one could reasonably expect the result to go the other way next time or the time after that. But if Notre Dame were to play a Division III school like Wesleyan University, that would always be a mismatch, since Wesleyan would never have a plausible chance to win. The difference in ability between the two teams, reflecting the difference in the two schools' commitment to football, would be too great. Even if Wesleyan was unbeaten that year, having pummeled Williams and Amherst and the rest, and even if Notre Dame was winless after having been beaten by USC and Penn State and the rest, only a fool in flat-front khakis and a cardinal-colored blazer would bet a penny on Wesleyan. It would take a miracle to even out the mismatch — an epidemic of spontaneous combustion along the Notre Dame sideline, say, or a Wesleyan running back acquiring the gift of flight.

The institutions of boxing are supposed to correct for life's natural inclination toward mismatches. State boxing commissions enforce the weight-class rules that provide the fight world's primary instrument for ensuring fair fights. (Allowing Notre Dame to field only players the same size as Wesleyan's would go far toward making a real game of their hypothetical encounter.) In addition to conducting weigh-ins, commissions also administer medical examinations, suspend injured or rule-breaking fighters, and, in theory, head off the worst mismatches. They are supposed to prevent a boxer who has been knocked cold three times in the past month from fighting in their jurisdiction, of course, but they are also supposed to make sure that a healthy but untried novice or an aging fifth-rater is not being lowered by the tail into a terrarium occupied by a proven world-beater who might just kill him. That still leaves plenty of acceptable variability, since fighters of comparable size and roughly commensurate ability may be faster or slower, thicker- or thinner-skulled, more or less ring-wise or well trained or pampered or mean.

In practice, since the boxing business cannot sequester itself entirely from the wider world and does not wish to, plenty of mismatches occur. Usually, a commission does no more than make sure that the combatants are about the same size and that nobody has kryptonite in his gloves. And, to be fair, why should a commission do more? It regulates fistic commerce, not human motivation. Everybody involved, not just the boxers but also their paying audience, can decide for himself or herself whether to participate. If consenting adults want to see an unfair fight, and if two mismatched fighters wish to sell their services in order to provide one, why should the boxing commission stand in the way?

One should keep in mind, too, that even boxers with grotesquely lopsided losing records know what they are doing. The lowliest of professional opponents — an every-time-out loser several rungs down the ladder from a hardy trial horse like Exum Speight — can fight better than almost everybody else on earth. Any one of them could beat the hell out of the typical top-flight contact-sports jock remotely his size, and any one of them could single-handedly clear out a bar full of fight-goers, writers, and other smart alecks who dismiss him as a stiff when he boxes in the ring.

Still, although you know that experts enter the ring of their own free will to practice their trade, watching a bad mismatch can make you feel sick. It seems worst when the better man is not good enough to get it over with. As the combatants labor around the ring, one swinging and the other ducking, you feel complicit in the wrongness of the event: the promoter's search for a sure-thing patsy to pad the favorite's record, the state commissioners' malign sloth, the audience's willingness to act as if it were being entertained by a contest of equals rather than a clumsy exhibition of butcher's work.

Maybe, also, a mismatch makes you feel sick because you put yourself in the fighters' places. Is the winner embarrassed? Is he enjoying himself? Has he deluded himself into believing that the other guy is a worthy opponent? I'm not sure which of these possibilities strikes me as the most awful. As for the loser, is he desperately trying to make it through the bout in one piece? Is he just marking time until he can go to his motel room and watch porn on TV? Has he deluded himself into believing that he has a chance to win and be champion someday? Perhaps in reaction to this unwelcome empathy, you start imagining an improbable reversal: the professional opponent's life-changing surge of purposeful rage, a sudden burst of sharp punching, the eerie hush of the crowd as the referee counts over the stunned favorite. When you catch yourself daydreaming like that, you can be sure you're watching a mismatch.

Usually, it's not hard to spot a mismatch. Either a fighter has a reasonable chance to win or he doesn't. It's not a matter of opinion. But the training of the eye of the beholder matters, too. Sometimes the logic of a mismatch — or, conversely, the logic of a fair fight that you expected to be a mismatch — comes clear only gradually, or after the fact. Learning to recognize that logic educates the ringsider's eye just as usefully as watching closely contested struggles between well-matched champions. Mismatches may be futile, wasteful, and not very entertaining (except to the sort of people it's best to avoid), but they can tell you a lot about boxing and about your capacity to see clearly through the distorting filters of sentiment, morbid curiosity, and a fascination with the exercise of power.

If you go regularly to club fights in smaller venues in and around Boston, you get used to seeing not only mismatches but also permutations of the same mismatch. The two main promoters of these cards in recent years, Rich Cappiello and Doug Pendarvis, tend to feed the same cheaply imported professional losers to the same local maulers. When I get to ringside before the evening's first fight, I look over the program to see how the usual suspects will be arranged this time. In the 125-to-135-pound range — featherweights and lightweights — I can expect to see Aaron "Two Guns" Torres of Brockton, Elio "The Destroyer" Rodriguez of Fitchburg, or Jeff "Hellraza" Fraza of Haverhill beat up one of the regular out-of-state punching bags, chief among whom of late have been Bobby "Too Sweet" Rishea, from Brantford, Ontario, and Rich "The Matador" Dinkins, from Mobile, Alabama.

On November 30, 2001, all five of them were on a Pendarvis card held at Lombardo's, a big ugly nightclub by the interstate in Randolph. There appeared to be four classic import-a-loser mismatches on the seven-fight card, to which Pendarvis had appended the title "Pride and Glory." Torres was slated to beat Dinkins, Rodriguez to beat Rishea. Within the past year, Dinkins had traveled north to New England to be knocked out in three or fewer rounds by four local fighters, including Torres in April and Fraza in January. In the same period, Rishea had come down from Canada to lose to three of the same four, including Torres. The two professional opponents were reliable in different ways: Dinkins, who had ten wins, nineteen losses, and two draws (with eleven losses and a draw in his last twelve fights), threw more punches and got knocked out more; Rishea, 2-16-2, played it safer and tended to lose by decision. Two other opponents on the card, both from North Carolina, appeared to be more out-of-state cannon fodder. Kevin Carter, a 6-21 welterweight who had recently lost two bouts to Boston fighters, was up against a straight-ahead bruiser from Stoughton named Eddie "Fightin' Irish" Bishop. And Andre Baker, 4-14-1, who had already lost by decision to Torres in August, looked as if he might develop into another 125-to-135-pound regular. He had been chosen as the human sacrifice in the headline bout against Fraza, a lightweight whose excitable backers from Haverhill were already filling up the front rows.

I knew the fighters' true records — scrupulously kept by a New Jersey company called Fight Fax, Inc. — because the state boxing commissioners, when they feel like doing at least part of their job properly, distribute copies of them to reporters and other ringsiders. The Fight Fax records can tell you everything necessary to spot a mismatch in the making before a single punch is thrown. Promoters regularly bend or falsify that information to encourage the paying audience to believe that it will see a fair fight. It's common practice for the ring announcer to tell the crowd something strategically nonspecific, if technically true — he may, for instance, introduce a guy with a record of 1-40 as "a battle-tested veteran of over forty tough pro contests" — and, especially at low-budget cards of only local consequence, the promoter will baldly lie to the customers about a record. Bobby Rishea, for instance, had been upgraded on Pendarvis's program to 4-8-2, double the true number of victories and half the losses. Sometimes the program tells one lie and the announcer tells a different one.

The first two scheduled mismatches went by the book. Rich Dinkins and Kevin Carter were, respectively, a white lightweight and a black welterweight variant of a type: a shaven-headed guy with muscles but no defense or offense. Both looked tough and threw a few wishful haymakers before covering up to last out their fights, which allowed supporters of Aaron Torres and Eddie Bishop to imagine, if they had another beer and squinted a little, that their man was getting the best of an opponent who could hurt him. Both favorites won all four rounds on all three judges' cards.

The third mismatch was two rounds longer and harder to watch. Pity curdles easily into contempt at the fights, and I always feel sorry for Bobby Rishea, a slight, balding, pale man with a tendency to turn red in odd, blotchy patterns, as if his opponents' gloves and the ropes were red-hot to the touch. Elio Rodriguez, an energetic young lightweight, teed off on him for six rounds. Rishea seemed to be struggling to be fully present, as if most of his will and strength were squandered in a losing internal battle to take control of his own body as it drifted around the ring. Rodriguez staggered him in the third round, but Rishea meekly craned his torso through the ropes to save himself. The referee — moved, perhaps, by the turtlelike honesty of that recourse, or by the livid blotches — stopped the action to let him recover. The bout went the distance, resulting in another shutout. Rishea, like Carter and Dinkins, had not won a single round on any judge's card, nor had any of them deserved to.

This kind of predictable futility can get depressing. The local guys were not world-beaters, but the professional opponents had no chance against them. In part, the difference came down to physical ability. Torres, Bishop, and Rodriguez could all hit at least moderately hard and kept the punches coming, and none of the opponents could get out of the way or hit back well enough to afford himself a chance to win. Dinkins had won eight fights by knockout in the distant past, but his punching had degenerated and his chin had softened since then. Carter could take a good punch, but didn't land any. Rishea could box a little, but his craft went almost exclusively toward surviving a round, not creating openings to score.

The futility went beyond differences in ability, though. Being paid to play a loser's role discourages professional opponents from taking drastic measures to mitigate a mismatch. Perhaps each of the three, if suitably inspired, might have found a way to maximize his strengths and minimize his weaknesses just enough to cause some trouble and make it a close fight, but why bother? The state commission's judges habitually awarded rounds to the local fighter even when he didn't deserve to win them, promoters might not invite an opponent back if he earned a reputation as a record-spoiler, and anyway, all three opponents were getting on in fighter-years past the point where a confirmed loser might ever be inspired to change his ways. I have trouble picturing Bobby Rishea looking in the bathroom mirror and saying to himself, "I can't go on like this. I will find a way to be 3-16-2, or die trying." And even if he did arrive at such a moment, it had been so long since he had won — six years — that he might not remember how to do it. Accepting a prospective mismatch can amount to tacitly throwing the fight: everybody, especially the participants, knows how it's supposed to turn out, which helps to ensure that there will be no surprises.

There was one scheduled mismatch to go, the evening's main event. It featured Jeff Fraza, a shove-and-haul advancer with a rabid hometown following and a padded record, a type in which Massachusetts seems to specialize these days. Busloads of yellow-T-shirted Team Fraza rooters from Haverhill came to his fights and howled for him with the special passion of people who feel themselves to have been cheated and sold short at every turn in life, but they will be damned if they let the same thing happen to their boy Hellraza. Like the dedicated supporters of Notre Dame's football team, who help it get invited to a bowl game even when it has had a so-so year, the enthusiastic sellout crowd that traveled with Fraza helped him get gigs as a headliner on local fight cards. A solid yellow front of zealots lined the route of his path to the ring at Lombardo's. When Fraza, a lizard-eyed little bruiser wearing glossy yellow sweats and a crude fade haircut, emerged from his dressing room for his ring walk, they got so excited I expected to hear ecstatic ululation. The opponent, Andre Baker, climbed into the ring almost unnoticed. Baker was one in-shape brother, trained down to knotty vulpine leanness, but he had lost a lot of fights.

I thought I would see more futility, but a closer reading of the official records would have told me that Fraza-Baker might not be a mismatch. Baker was indeed 4-14-1, but he had been matched tough, as they say, to a fault. He had fought only two men with losing records, and one making his pro debut, and had beaten all three. The others had been prolific winners, most of them unbeaten when they fought Baker, which amounted to absurdly stiff competition. Baker went the hard way: he usually fought outside his home state, he fought southpaws, he fought rematches against unbeaten opponents. His father trained and managed him, which suggested a misguided insistence on honing the son against stern competition, rather than cynical exploitation. Whatever the opposite of coddled is, Baker was that. Fraza, by contrast, was 10-1 with six knockouts, but none of his opponents had entered the ring with a winning record, not even the one who beat him. It said nothing good about Fraza that he had been knocking out opponents like Rich Dinkins and Gerry Ocampo, an in-state patsy from Holyoke who was 1-34-2 when Fraza fought him. Fraza, not Baker, would be the one stepping up in quality of opposition in the main event.

There was one other factor in Baker's favor that I might have taken into account in assessing the matchup, but I found out about it only after the fight. Earlier in the evening, when the Bakers arrived at the venue, a sympathetic reporter had asked Baker's father if they had ever seen Fraza in action. No, they hadn't; they hadn't even seen any tape. The reporter, feeling that Baker deserved a break and Fraza didn't, told Baker's father that Fraza was too slow and punched too wide to hurt anybody who had a little speed, stamina, and boxing skill. Just keep moving and jabbing him, the reporter advised, and plan to throw a counter whenever he punches; Fraza will wear out. The father said thanks.

The main event was no mismatch. Fraza stalked, trying to pen Baker in a corner, while Baker moved and countered, trying to score while frustrating Fraza. Fierce but occluded, like a radio tuned just shy of a heavy metal station, Fraza did not land many clean blows, even though he attacked furiously whenever he could. Baker had little punching power, but when he caught Fraza coming in — adding Fraza's momentum to the force of the blow — he could jar him. The rounds were close; I had the fight scored even at the halfway point. The Haverhill tribe made their exhortatory noise, but a troubled note had entered into it. Rich Cappiello, who was not promoting this card but who often promotes Fraza's fights, seemed concerned, too. Cappiello, a bodybuilder who usually has a fresh haircut and a tan, left his front-row seat after the fifth round to visit Fraza's corner, where he told his man to pick it up and hit the fucking guy. Fraza kept chasing and punching, but he tired. Baker, meanwhile, seemed to get quicker and more resourceful. He nailed Fraza with a draining body shot in the seventh, his best punch of the fight, and he circled away, jabbing, in the eighth as Fraza desperately tried to reach him before the final bell.

I had scored the fight a draw. Baker had boxed well, but I thought that Fraza had won four rounds through sheer persistent aggression and volume of punching, enough to pull out a draw. I checked with Mike Nosky, the reporter seated on my left, and he had it the same way: 76-76. We figured the judges would give it to Fraza by the usual hometown landslide, this being Massachusetts, but they surprised us. One of them did indeed award Fraza a 78-75 gift, but the other two scored it 77-75 for Baker, who exulted in the ring as if he had won the title. Fraza had been humiliated in front of his people, who made outraged noises but did not resort to throwing things. You could almost hear them thinking, in an undercurrent running beneath their vocal anger at the decision, that maybe their guy hadn't looked so good against an opponent who knew how to fight back, that maybe the invincible Hellraza was another bill of goods they had been sold. Across the ring, Rich Cappiello was shouting, "Fuckin' *judges! Fuck* them!" He stormed over to Nick Manzello, the chairman of the state commission, and demanded to know what a guy had to do to get a hometown decision anymore around here.

Ringsiders are supposed to refrain from pestering the judges about their decisions, but I was surprised enough to turn to the judge seated on my right, a state police lieutenant named Leo Gerstel, and ask him what he had been thinking. After all, I was no Massachusetts homer and I had only called it a draw, not a win for Baker. Gerstel, a capable-looking gent who won the state Golden Gloves title as a small heavyweight a long time ago, was one of the two judges who had scored the bout in Baker's favor. He had dismounted from his high stool and was hurriedly packing up his papers and putting on his jacket while keeping an eye on Cappiello, who was still yelling into the chairman's sagging, deep-lined face on the other side of the ring. "Look," said Gerstel, "if the kid has the courage to come here and fight that guy in front of the hometown fans, I should have the courage to call it like it was." Then he excused himself and slipped out a side door.

In Fraza's dressing room, the defeated favorite slumped

on a folding chair. His cornermen, including his father, moved around with exaggerated care, as if in a sickroom. Pressed by reporters, Fraza admitted that he should have jabbed more, as his father and everyone else had urged him to do, and he said he had to accept his defeat and move on. Then he made some excuses: he was still recovering from a car accident he'd had over the summer; Baker ran away and the referee should have forced him to stand and fight. (Almost every puncher who has been outboxed says that the other guy ran away and that the ref should have done something about it.) He said he thought he had done enough to pull out a victory, or at least a draw. "But I don't get no breaks," he added, "so I didn't expect it." Twisting up his face as if tasting something spoiled, he said, "In the state of Massachusetts . . . ," but he let the thought trail off. It would not do to complain to reporters that the outsider, not the local, was supposed to get robbed. "I still am going to be world champion, though. I know that. Guaranteed." His father nodded grimly. Somebody came in to announce that a couple of Haverhill rooters they all knew had been arrested in the parking lot. The police were forcing the milling faithful to leave soon, so Fraza would have to hurry if he wanted to catch one of the rented buses going home. "I'm not riding with those fucking animals," he said.

In the winner's dressing room, Baker's father did most of the talking. (First, he gave a big hug to the reporter who had sized up Fraza for him. It puzzled me at the time.) Andre, sitting on a table in his underwear, dangling his bare legs, was grinning and saying "Yeah, boy, we did it" into a cell phone. Meanwhile, his father, speaking in the trainer's traditional first-person plural, explained the victory: "We stood with our game plan. We said, 'Let's not overdo it. Let him come to us.'" He felt vindicated in his practice of matching his son tough. "Going the distance with good guys," he said, "it's gonna put him where they are." So far, Andre's career had been a disaster, but his handling of Fraza suggested that he had learned something from all those difficult fights. Perhaps his fortunes were turning upward at last. Andre put down the phone and said to nobody in particular, "You put one win together with another, and you can be champion of the world." His father nodded, smiling. Andre was 5-14-1.

Before Baker fought Fraza, during a break between undercard bouts earlier in the evening, Leo Gerstel told me about fetching people out of the water. Gerstel, the judge who was also a state trooper, commanded the underwater rescue unit. He said that everything depended on the "golden hour," the variable time a person can survive while submerged and unconscious. The deeper and colder the water, and the younger you are, the better chance you have. But it's always a long shot. "Usually it's recovery," he said, "not rescue." When Baker talked after the fight about contending for a title, I allowed myself to wonder if he, already twenty-eight years old and twenty fights into his career, could possibly be rescued in time from the fate of the professional opponent.

The answer was no. His victory over Fraza and his brutal seasoning against good fighters might allow him to be

matched a step higher, and he could always dream of getting attention by miraculously upsetting a ranked contender, but the only promotion in status he could plausibly
expect would be slightly improved paydays and more talented foes who were more likely to hurt him. He had heart
and some craft, but not power, which meant he would
never pose a threat to a good fighter, and his father's matchmaking philosophy would never allow him to even up his
record against not-so-good ones. The habit of losing had
been ingrained in him (and he would lose his next fight, in
which, predictably, his father matched him tough). But on
that November night in Randolph, when he found it in
himself to outbox a hometown favorite and two judges
found it in themselves to reward him for a job well done, he
could believe that the golden hour had not elapsed.

I told you that modestly uplifting story of a mismatch-that-
wasn't so I could tell you this: sometimes a mismatch-
that-was can be uplifting, too. It happens — rarely, but
not never — that you come away from a terribly unfair
fight with a profound feeling of rightness, a sense of having been afforded a fugitive insight into life's normally
inscrutable symmetry. The most upliftingly unfair fistic
mismatch I ever saw was a street fight outside a bar in Middletown, Connecticut, in 1984. A three-on-one affair, at
least at first, it could never have taken place in a boxing
ring, not even on the Massachusetts state commission's
blinky watch.

I saw the fight long enough ago, in an impressionable

moment when I was on the cusp of adulthood, that my memory of it has become a sort of fairy tale I tell myself from time to time. It happened on one of those transitional nights in the first weeks of the fall semester, when the waning gentleness of the air already inspires nostalgia for summer. A handful of students from Wesleyan (including me) and a scattering of locals were drinking with no great urgency at John B.'s, a bar on one of the narrow side streets that slant down toward the river from Middletown's Main Street. John B.'s was the kind of sweaty, droopy place, found near campuses all over America, that students and professors regard as a town joint and that locals regard as overrun by college types.

Sitting on stools at the bar were a couple of notorious characters from Wesleyan, the Count and his Henchman, attended by a satellite, the Fellow Traveler. The Count was the kind of guy who, upon being deposited in front of his freshman dorm on the first day of college with floor lamp, hockey sticks, and a blue blazer already too tight in the shoulders, suddenly realizes how far physical competence and self-possession can take him among harmless, still unformed classmates. Bandy-legged and improbably muscular, radiating selfish dynamism, he had swiftly discovered that almost none of them would stand up to him. Flourishing in the role of campus villain, he had metamorphosed into the Count, a devil-may-care brigand who feared nothing and lived only to add exploits to his rap sheet: tearing off a woman's shirt at a party, climbing up the outside wall of a dorm to harass and despoil its inhabitants, leading a late-night assault on the quad in which a pothead was whacked in the eye with a hockey stick. As always happens in these cases, his swashbuckling aura attracted followers, broad-shouldered young men of weak character who found themselves, true to type, vying for his favor and chortling nefariously while perpetrating misdeeds. First among these was the Henchman, a helmet-haired blond lout (reputed to have wielded the hockey stick in the pothead-beaning incident), who was larger than the Count but lacked the spark of inspiration.

Astride his barstool on a slow weeknight, joking with his retainers, the Count should have been beginning his junior year, but he had been suspended for the semester after a couple of scrapes with the college authorities. Perhaps the suspension helped maroon him in a state of in-betweenness — between student and nonstudent, summer and fall, the kid from Massachusetts he had been and the outsize character from central casting he had become — which encouraged him to forget that in the local bars he might encounter a different class of opponents.

Sudden pounding and then a sharp crack from the back of the room made everyone in the place look up in time to see the Henchman wrenching the flimsy bathroom door off its hinges. Apparently it had been locked from inside and he had grown impatient with the need to void. Surprised but pleased after the fact to have broken the door, he was just beginning to consider what to do next when a thick, hairy guy came out of the bathroom and shouldered him aside. They exchanged strong words. The Henchman, still holding the detached door by the handle, called out the Count's Christian name in a peculiar singsong voice. The hairy guy from the bathroom inspected the Henchman, then the Count, then the Fellow Traveler, weighing the business at hand against the moment in which he confronted it.

Had it been mid-July, with almost all the students gone and the college well into its annual dormant phase in the life of the town, the hairy guy would probably have taken advantage of the Henchman's belligerent but unready posture — muscles flexed, hands down — to drill him then and there on the bridge of the nose, knocking him across the room and into next week. Had it been late October, when the place might be filled with college students under a full head of fall-semester steam (in which case he would almost certainly not have been there at all), the hairy guy would probably have let it go with a final hard look. But, on the cusp of seasons, he considered briefly, then jerked a thumb toward the bar's front door and said in a low but penetrating voice, "That's it. All of you. Outside." There was a note of fatherly rigor in it: *Get me a hickory switch and drop them pants.* Without waiting to see what they would do, he stalked across the room and out the door.

The notorious characters considered the invitation. The guy was not as big as the Henchman; he was barrel-chested and broad-limbed, but he was no body-sculpted weightlifter like the Count; and if he was bigger than the Count and the Fellow Traveler (who, physically, was a three-quarter-size copy of the Count), it was not by much. He was closer to forty than thirty, with a significant paunch and fierce, curly dark hair growing on every exposed inch of his body except his forehead, nose, and eyes. Paunch and hair were abundantly on view because he wore only jeans, gym shoes, and a sort of puffy safari vest. His features had a Mediterranean cast — Greek, perhaps, or Turkish, although in Middletown Sicilian was a better bet. He might work for the local concrete company, or in construction; perhaps he had done a stint in the merchant marine. More important, he had been drinking in a desperately dull bar on a weeknight, and should have been left in peace to do that. The notorious characters smiled uncertainly at one another, anticipating an adventure, as they rolled their shoulders and prepared to follow him outside. That their prospective opponent was already pacing up and down in the street, alternately cracking his knuckles and shaking both fists overhead while bellowing "I am the Terminator" (as far as those inside could make out through the bar's windows), should have given them greater pause, but they weren't used to dealing with people like him. They moved toward the door.

They were intercepted by the Sage, a lean, shaven-headed, thirtyish black man in gold wire-frame glasses and a tight brown shirt, who said, "Fellas, I wouldn't go out there if I was you." Having read the Fight Fax records written all over their bodies and manner, he could see through their advantage in numbers to recognize that they were on the short end of the coming mismatch. That entitled them to a warning, if not sympathy. The Sage had the dispassionate air of an outdoorsman pausing in his descent of a storm-prone mountain to point out the late hour and sinking temperature to a trio of robust novices in shorts, carrying only six-packs of beer, just beginning the ascent. The notorious characters exchanged a long look with him, then stepped to one side and huddled briefly, as if they had called time out. There was a chance they might get seriously hurt, but they might get the better of the man outside, put him down and hurt him. Since he was not a fellow student, they would be able to go further, perhaps much further than they ever had before, in hurting him. Or maybe there would just be a good set-to among equals, a rough scrimmage, at the end of which the Terminator would acknowledge by word or gesture that he and they were all of a kind — piratical fellows who got in fights at bars and afterward hoisted drinks with warlike joy.

Had it been mid-July, they probably would have decided that the Terminator was too forbidding to fight on his home turf. Had it been late October, they probably would have decided that there was too much fun to be had on campus, too many submissive peers and too much free beer, to risk getting dragged into a potentially complicated entanglement in town. In either case, they would have turned back to the bar, had another drink, and tried to laugh about the fuming townie waiting for them out in the street. Later, when it became a story they told, they would have laughed at themselves, too, and at what a close call they'd had. But now, on the cusp of seasons, they could not find their bearings. Meanwhile, the interrupted drinkers in the bar, students and locals alike, were exerting a silent pressure to go through with the fight. We wanted to see what would happen.

Rushed and uncertain, the notorious characters made a mistake. They broke their huddle, brushed dismissively past the Sage, and went out into the street. He sighed and posted himself by the door to watch. The ringside spectators, seated comfortably with drinks at hand, observed the rest of the action through the bar's wide plate-glass window and three small, upright rectangular windows set in the front door.

What followed was not so much a fight as a kind of reasoned exposition, like a lecture, in which an elegant chain of assertions supported by incontrovertible evidence was hammered out on the students' faces. While the Count was still peeling off his tight white T-shirt to reveal his astoundingly well-developed torso, and while the Henchman was following suit, the Fellow Traveler walked over to the Terminator, apparently to have a word with him, perhaps even to head off hostilities. This was also a mistake. As soon as the Fellow Traveler, the smallest and best-natured of the Count's faction, got within range, grinning and holding his open hands high and palms-forward in the traditional "let's have a little talk, big fella" gesture, the Terminator punched him, a concise right hand thrown with lots of tight-sprung force and the elbow turned out just before impact. It was a big fist and it mashed most of the left side of the Fellow Traveler's face. He stiffened and dove out of sight, cut off from view by the plate-glass window's lower frame. The Count appeared, shirtless and bulging, received a couple of punches in the nose — a left, which seemed to be thrown for variety's sake, and then a mirror-image right — and reeled abruptly backward out of the side of the frame. The Terminator advanced on the Henchman, the two disappearing from view between the big window and those in the door. Offstage, so to speak, the Henchman got his medicine as well.

The Fellow Traveler came back into the bar, approached a student he knew, and asked, "Does my face look funny?" Informed that the left side of it had inflated, which made the uninjured side look like a flat tire, he said, "He's really tough," with swollen-lipped conviction. Then he sat by the window to watch the rest of the affray. Meanwhile, the Count and the Henchman each had another go at the Terminator, who belted them aside, each in his turn.

Everyone knew that the fight, as a fight, was over. There had already been a weary, let's-get-this-over-with quality to the Count's and the Henchman's second assaults. They now understood the decisive difference between themselves and the Terminator — he knew about fighting, while they knew about rough games and mauling incompetent victims — but they had invested too much in their personas to give up without first taking a beating. That, and the presence of an audience, prevented them from running away up the street back to campus. Perhaps, too, they counted on the Terminator's sense of fistic proportion to rein him in. He did not seem like the sort of gratuitously cruel street fighter who would put the boot to a downed man, although he would certainly keep whacking anybody who did not stay down.

There was a pause in the action, during which the Sage appeared to reach a decision and went outside. The bartender moved briskly to the door and double-locked it behind him. The Count, who had been lying in the street in a semi-fetal position, got unsteadily to his feet. The Sage went to him and beat him up while managing to communicate a nose-holding distaste for having to touch somebody so bloody and gross. The spectators came to appreciate that the Sage, sinewy where the Terminator was thick, was also a fast and expert puncher. He did not hit as hard as the Terminator, but the Count was already dazed and went to one knee without putting up a fight. The set of his shoulders and lowered head seemed to say, *Okay, enough, I get the point.*

The Henchman appeared at the little windows in the door, which he rattled for a while before realizing it would not open. A new expressiveness animated his manner. His bugging eyes, sincere diction (amenable to lip-reading even by amateurs), and hand gestures — the left tipped to his ear with thumb and pinkie splayed, the right bunched and held up under his chin with index finger jabbing insistently downward at the latch — mimed his passionate wish that the bartender call the police and unlock the door immediately. (It occurs to me now that he still had to go to the bathroom, too.)

In midperformance, the Henchman was jerked from view by an unseen hand and reappeared with his back to the plate-glass window. The Terminator advanced calmly upon him, feinted expertly with his right, and, when the Henchman flinched away in a posture of entreaty, hit him with a couple of sharp but comparatively light left jabs, each of which snapped back the Henchman's head and caused him to retreat one step. When he had framed the Henchman in front of the window with his left, like tapping a nail to get it started in the wood, he threw the right, driving the nailhead flush to the wood with one blow. The back of the Henchman's blond head bounced hard off the window, making a rich, thrumming boom that profoundly impressed the spectators inside, who exchanged odd confirmatory glances, as if earlier in the evening they had been discussing what it sounds like when somebody's head bounces off plate glass without breaking it.

Stumbling but still on his feet, the Henchman slid laterally along the glass and disappeared from view. The Terminator went after him. Those in the bar could follow their progress by the sound the Henchman's head made as it rocketed off the building's outer wall somewhere between the window and the door. After a few repetitions the noise stopped. The Terminator and the Sage knocked politely on the door, were admitted with publican flair by the bartender, and resumed their seats and drinks.

After an interval, the Count and the Henchman came back in to avoid the cops, who screeched up in a blast of lights and sirens. The Count's nose was a pulsating knot of aggrieved tissue, snot, and blood, some of which had splattered in a jet down his bare chest. He seemed oddly jaunty,

almost thankful to have gotten a beating in the way that
bullies can be. With a wry expression on his swollen face,
he returned to the bar to drain his half-filled stein of beer in
one gulp before the cops got to him. Two of them entered
and took a firm grip on his plump biceps to haul him out.
More cops arrived. Sensibly, they rounded up the half-na-
ked guys who looked like they had been in a fight. The Terminator and the Sage, whose only injuries had been to the
skin of their knuckles, claimed to be innocent bystanders;
the arrestees did not gainsay them. The notorious characters found themselves in a schoolyard bind: they regarded
telling the cops the truth as finking and therefore beneath
them, but on the other hand it wasn't fair that the winners
didn't have to go to jail. The small-town cops, who had to
put up with too much from college students in general
and these students in particular, and who had immediately
grasped and approved of the scene's nuances, scotched this
developing moral crisis by letting the winners go and advis-
ing the losers to shut up.

After the police cruisers had taken away the collegians,
the Terminator and the Sage finished their drinks and de-
parted. There was no applause from the spectators, but it
was implied in the tailing off of already muted conversations that marked the victors' exit. They parted ways after
crossing the threshold of the front door, one going left and
the other right.

Through the window we could see the Terminator trudg-
ing alone uphill toward Main Street into a stiffening
breeze, fists jammed in the pockets of his puffy vest, seem-

ingly in the grip of postpugilistic tristesse. When he had disappeared from view, leaving an empty scene across which the curtain should momentarily fall or the credits commence to roll, everyone could feel the change, like the great steel door of a bank vault swinging shut, its time locks whirring and clicking: summer was over.

Andre Baker had to suffer for his father's optimistic view of an ass-whipping's didactic value, but the father might well have been right to believe that the son could absorb some of the potency of the fighters who defeated him in mismatches. Did the Count and his followers come away from their defeat clutching at least a shard of the Terminator's (and the Sage's) ability and good fighting sense? Perhaps, although it would only have made them more accomplished punks. I wish I could tell you that they spent the rest of their college careers protecting bookish types from miscreants and carrying sophomore virgins in adorably decorated leg casts across busy streets, but they went along pretty much the same as before, throwing their weight around on campus. If anything, they had been reminded at John B.'s to pick on the weak and let the strong be.

What else could they have learned? For one thing, they could have picked up some pointers on method. The Terminator probably had not boxed formally, but he might have knocked around the bags some, and his sound mechanics and expert eye for sizing up opposition indicated that he had been in fights before. He had admirable punching form, relaxed and direct, and once the hitting started he did not waste any motion on chest-puffing, shoving and cursing, and other stage business that distracts college he-men from the business of winning a fight. As far as I could tell, the Terminator presented a perfect model of efficiency: he landed every punch he threw, and his opponents did not land even one. He also knew to take multiple opponents one at a time, if they let him, applying his full attention to each in turn. The Count's crew obliged by coming at him singly in sequence, with the ignorant chivalry of novices whose model of fighting derived from sports rather than work. Their only chance to even up the mismatch would have been in ganging together to bring him down. Next time they had a dangerous hitter outnumbered, they might know to exploit their advantage in numbers, although it was more likely that next time they would remember what had happened at John B.'s and decline the opportunity to step up in class of competition.

What if, as in the case of Baker's defeat of Fraza, the ap-parent mismatch had gone the other way? What if the Count and his boys had fought more intelligently and en-joyed some miraculous piece of luck and somehow beaten the Terminator, or at least held him to a draw?

At the time, that result would have been deeply dispirit-ing to me. Having built their careers on a series of terrible mismatches in their favor, the college bullies were overdue for the comeuppance they received. I came away from the bar that night with a novel appreciation for the subtle clockwork order of the universe. The elaborate concatena-tion of righteous circumstance that had brought together the principals in the evening's drama could give a guy religion, or at least a new faith in natural justice. The advantages enjoyed by Wesleyan students — money, good health care, youth, prospects, the sheltering bulwarks of their parents' social position and the college's endowment — did not count for much in a street fight (although they would if doctors and lawyers became involved afterward). To the contrary, the momentum of the college boys' privilege only added to the force of the Terminator's shots when he caught them coming in, wide open and expecting another easy conquest. Their undoing struck me as gorgeously symmetrical. During the long, high-shouldered walk up the hill from Main Street to my room late that night, I was warmed — for perhaps the first time in my sort-of-adult life — by the feeling that all was right with the world.

But now, almost twenty years after, looking back on that comeuppance in light of hundreds of state commission–approved mismatches at which I have been present since then, I am less uplifted by it. I am even a bit dispirited by the realization that the parable of just desserts that I have treasured for so long amounts to another futility-soaked repetition of a now familiar routine: the competent crushing the incompetent. I have to admit that now, as a student of the fights, I might even regard an unlikely upset victory by the Count's faction as uplifting, too, perhaps just as uplifting as the storybook beating they received. They profoundly deserved the beating on moral grounds, true, and they had a seemingly unfair advantage in numbers, but even so they were prohibitive underdogs in the fight, as outclassed as

Andre Baker or Bobby Rishea usually is. That means they would have had to rise well above themselves in finding a way to triumph over the mismatch they faced. They would have had to discover some hidden mettle in themselves and to learn on the fly from the Terminator himself, even while hotly engaged with his superior ability, even as he made them suffer. That would have been something rare, and inspiring, to see.

4

An Appetite for Hitting

PEOPLE LIKE to touch fighters, especially retired fighters.
Men clap them on the shoulder, linger over a handshake.
Women have a habit of laying a hand intimately on a fighter's upper arm. Nothing so crude as squeezing a biceps, it
looks more like a preliminary to taking ballroom dance position. Laying hands on a fighter, lifelong noncombatants
can feel the force that has flowed through him in the form
of blows given and taken. It's like putting your hand on a
smoothbore cannon and imagining you can feel resonances
of a long-ago war.

At Washington's City Club in October 1999, on the
night before Fight Night — a yearly event for children's
charities sponsored by Fight for Children — a select inner
circle of patrons mingled with eminent retired fighters who

performed their roles with extra gentleness because they were in town to support a good cause. Ken Norton and Iran Barkley stooped and smiled, as big men will do when trying not to scare off children. Jake La Motta, the one-time middleweight champion now famous mostly for having been played in a movie by Robert De Niro, deadpanned old jokes with a practiced vaudevillian air. Smokin' Joe Frazier left off posing for pictures with well-wishers to sing a short set of soul chestnuts with White Smoke, his band from Philadelphia. Frazier's voice has an affecting huskiness, but when he strains and drifts flat he sounds like Larry Holmes, another singing former champion of whom it has been said that he should not quit his day job. Frazier seemed to address his showstopper, a pugilistically reworded version of "My Way," to Barkley, who stood on his heels to one side, smiling quizzically.

Earnie Shavers, the anvil-fisted heavyweight terror of the 1970s, sat at a table with a black marker in his right hand, signing the red imitation boxing gloves that guests received at the door for the purpose of collecting autographs. He had moved to England, where he worked the after-dinner speaking circuit and helped train a light heavyweight named Kenny Rainford, but he had flown in for Fight Night. Shaven-headed and courtly in a blue suit, Shavers signed gloves for men who laughed too much and for stylish society matrons who perched in the chair next to him for a moment, placed a hand lightly on his arm, and smiled into his eyes.

Even people who have never spoken to a fighter before,

and probably never will again, like to call ex-champions "champ," an honorific enjoyed in perpetuity, like "Admiral" or "Governor." Formal and slightly archaic, "champ" just appears in the mouth of the speaker, who seems a bit embarrassed but pleasantly surprised to find it there. All of the distinguished retirees at the City Club answered to "champ," except Shavers. For all his punching power, and although he compiled a record of 73-14-1 that included sixty-seven victories by knockout, he never held the title. He never did master the art of combination punching, the lack of mystery in his style made him too hittable, and he had recurring stamina problems because he had trouble relaxing in the ring. Too often he fought tight, so keyed up to kill the other guy with one punch that he burned up his own reserves of energy. At his bomb-throwing best he could still be had by a master boxer like Larry Holmes or Muhammad Ali, both of whom weathered his pounding and beat him. He overpowered the shifty defensive tactician Jimmy Young and the tough guy Roy "Tiger" Williams, and he blasted out both Jimmy Ellis and Ken Norton in the first round, but the hardheaded Jerry Quarry knocked him out; so did Ron Lyle, another bruiser, in a memorable punchers' ball during which Shavers and Lyle lambasted each other from bell to bell for six rounds. Once his best days had passed and Shavers slipped from contender to high-end trial horse, he got knocked out by second-tier contenders like Tex Cobb and Bernardo Mercado.

Most of the guests knew little or nothing about Shavers's fights, or about boxing at all. But they were drawn to

Shavers anyway, as they were drawn to all the retired fighters, by the vestige of force that surrounded him like a tang of cordite woven into the room-filling bouquet of good cigars and expensively tended skin and hair.

The next day, Shavers went to lunch at the lobby restaurant of the Washington Hilton and Towers, which hosts Fight Night every year. Passing through the lobby, he ran into Hector "Macho" Camacho, the veteran middleweight who would be co-headlining the evening's fight card. Camacho has cultivated celebrity by masking a potentially unmarketable talent for avoiding punches with flamboyant showmanship and an aggressively unpredictable manner. Camacho, unlike Shavers and most other fighters, walks around as if spoiling for a fight. Wrapped in loose sweats, he looked big for a middleweight, thick-necked, with the extra blockiness that some lean men acquire in their thirties. He has a blunt handsomeness common to charismatic bullies, punctuated by a provoking little curl he cultivates at the front of his cropped hairline.

At lunchtime, only hours before his bout, Camacho restlessly trolled the Hilton's lobby for diversion, trailing a coterie of seconds. His manager was saying, "Come on, champ, get off your feet, come on and sit," but Camacho, rattling with energy, could not keep still. Encountering Shavers, Camacho said, "He-e-eyyy," and pointed with both index fingers. Shavers smiled and said, "Hey champ," raising a fist in a gesture that was half punch and half exhortation, but he didn't stop to chat. Once he was past

Camacho, Shavers's smile altered and he made a doubtful face. He said, "I don't know about that guy. He's a good fighter and all, but when I was in camp training for a fight I spent eighteen hours a day in bed. No alcohol, no drugs, no women. Look at him. What's he doing out here? He's fighting *tonight*."

Shavers worked hard at the puncher's craft, and he hit as hard as anybody ever did. The only puncher of his time — or perhaps of any era — who might have claimed to be in his league was the young George Foreman, but Foreman had a wasteful, wide-swinging style. Shavers threw straighter, crisper blows. "I don't think George hit harder," Shavers said at lunch, picking at his fruit plate. "George was more clubbing, he used more arm, more of a sweeping motion. I was more direct." Larry Holmes, talking about Shavers on the phone from his office in Easton a few days later, agreed: "I never fought Foreman, but I'd say Shavers hit harder. Earnie was more direct. He had better form. When I first heard I had to fight him, I said, 'Why I got to fight that man?' I didn't want to get hit by him." Holmes knew he could hit Shavers, because defense had never been Shavers's forte. "He always carried his hands too close," Holmes said. "Couldn't keep the punches off of himself." He meant that Shavers kept his gloves tucked against his head, in firing position, rather than extending his arms to interrupt incoming punches before they took final form. "Didn't make me feel better about fighting him, though. I still didn't want to get hit by him."

Shavers believes that punching power is mostly a gift.

"You can't teach real power," he said, spearing a section of orange, "not to somebody doesn't have any, but you can improve what you've got. You can exercise, like this fighter I work with, I have him chop trees to build up his back and legs. I grew up working on a farm, throwing bales of hay, wheat. Lots of repetitions, but not a lot of weight. Makes you strong." Shavers, like many other fight people of his generation who think that pumping iron impairs speed and suppleness, prefers manual labor to working out as a way to build strength. "And you can improve power by working on technique," he continued, "twisting and stopping the body, *snapping* the body, for that six-inch punch."

Pressed for details, he pushed back his chair, rose from the table, and threw a couple of sample punches in the air. At fifty-four, his form was still balanced and fluid: legs planted and flexed, chin tucked in, bulky torso turning on the pivot of the waist to put weight into the blow, the whole crushing motion forcefully initiated and sharply arrested. The jacket of his blue suit flew open, his smooth brown head caught the lights, his face fell into a practiced scowl of concentration. Shavers is a hale, friendly man, blessed with a gracious disposition and a tee-hee laugh that take the edge off his imposing appearance, but when he threw a punch he looked like the wrath of God.

Downstairs, in the International Ballroom, workers were setting up the ring and sound system for Fight Night. The evening would be one long show, with fighters, singers, dancers, hostesses, servers, and guests all in character and in costume, enacting their parts. Camacho would be one of the featured performers: boxing is, after all, a staged spectacle intended to entertain. But boxing is also something far more elemental — a negotiation of force, a matter of hitting and being hit — that goes deeper than the layers of show business in which it is wrapped. On Fight Night, Shavers's long history of hitting, of naked force, would be dressed up in the dignified role of a warrior who has forsaken arms as he and the other retirees made their way through the evening's scripted acts — the prefatory cocktail parties, the dinner, the introductory song and dance in the ring, and then the fights.

All afternoon and evening, the players gathered at the Hilton. When Shavers went to get a shoeshine after lunch he ran into Eric Esch, better known as Butterbean, the zeppelinesque heavyweight from Jasper, Alabama, featured in the evening's other headline bout. Butterbean leaned against a pillar in the lobby, wearing jeans and a short black jacket with writing on it, looking for all the world like an extra-wide regular guy waiting for a bus. But then a blond hotel guest approached him and asked if her husband could take a picture of her with him. She shyly nestled up to Butterbean and he obliged with an arm around her and a big smile, but the husband couldn't get the camera to work properly, so Butterbean was stranded in the prolonged clinch until Shavers came along to save him. As the two fighters shook hands and exchanged good wishes, Butterbean's huge, pale, hairless skull nodded toward and almost touched Shavers's brown dome.

A pack of impossibly fit and fresh-looking young women arrived, all about the same size, in red-and-white warmups. These were the Redskinettes, the Washington Redskins' cheerleaders. They waited while a straggler caught up. She had come in a different entrance and gotten lost in the hotel, but she was wearing a headset telephone and somebody talked her down to the lobby, not unlike the way the guy in the control tower tells the stewardess how to fly the plane in a disaster movie. When the straggler had been recovered, the Redskinettes continued down to the ballroom level to get ready. They found an empty hallway in which to rehearse their routine of strenuously feline maneuvers, all executed while smiling and not appearing to breathe heavily. Male hotel employees seemed to be contriving errands that took them down this hallway.

The average height of the women passing through the lobby increased by several inches as the hostesses began streaming in. Made-up and coifed as if for a war party, uniformly leggy, decked out in a variety of eye-catching evening wear, they strode, swayed, and clattered along on deadly-looking high heels. Fight Night's organizers had hired the Erickson Agency to supply appealing female company for the male patrons. The hostesses were paid a standard rate of $55 per hour to look good and see to the gentlemen's needs for food, drink, cigars, and platonic attention. In the spirit of Fight Night, the hostesses returned up to half their wages to Fight for Children as charitable donations. These women were for the most part professionals in the babe trade — models and actresses, broadly construed. Like the Redskinettes, they had spent significant portions of their lives passing up dessert and doing situps, but the hostesses were trained down almost too fine, to gauntness. Towering in their heels, they made the more compactly built Redskinettes look like shapely dwarfs.

The public relations crew managing the Fight Night show had been running around the hotel all day, murmuring into cell phones and sheepdogging retired fighters. Now, having changed into formal wear, they gathered in the lobby, a cluster of men in tuxedos and a couple of women in black and red dresses. They were keyed up, ready to go; the guests would be arriving soon.

The greeters deployed in the lobby. These were women wearing red satin shorts, sleeveless white Everlast tops, and black half-gloves of the kind used by boxers when they hit bags in training. They huddled around their boss, Tricia Erickson, a tall blond in a white dress, who reminded them of the game plan. "The guests will come in through these outside doors here. You say, 'Welcome to Fight Night,' cheerful, full of energy, and then you say, 'Right this way.'" Here she modeled an arm gesture worthy of a figure skater, with elements of both pointing and flourish in it, directed toward the stairs. She posted the greeters in a skirmish line across the lobby and then rushed downstairs to attend to the main body of her troops massing on the ballroom level.

In the enormous International Ballroom, scores of black-clad servers were setting 189 round tables arranged concentrically around a raised ring. In the ring, the Pointer Sisters rehearsed their mini-set, two numbers they would sing over a taped music track. The timing of their entrance needed work. They had to climb through the ropes, greet the audience, and be ready to sing "I'm So Excited" on cue. If they were too slow, they would have to start singing while still negotiating the ropes; if they got into the ring too soon, they would be forced to stall until the singing cue, giving the audience occasion to consider the fact that they were doing a karaoke version of their own song. Practicing their spontaneous greetings, the Pointer Sisters shouted "Hello!" and "Yeah, Fight Night!" as if the servers and technicians in the ballroom were cheering instead of going about their business. When the sound check was done, they climbed out of the ring again and the music cut off. One server, a broad-beamed woman of middle years with a napkin over her arm, could be heard saying to a colleague, "Macho Camacho's still fighting? With his old-ass self? Who's he fighting?"

The guests, the patrons of Fight for Children, began to arrive. Two thousand strong, they had donated up to $25,000 apiece, for a total of $2 million, making Fight Night one of the biggest charity events in town. They were, for the most part, rich and powerful businessmen, lawyers, politicos. Most lived in the Washington area, but some came from other states or countries every year for Fight Night. And they were, almost without exception, men: old ones and almost young ones, fat and thin, they all tended to good haircuts, fresh shaves, and crisp tuxedos. It being early, their bow ties were still on straight.

"There will be five seated women this year, and I'm one of them," said Alexis Contant, executive director of Fight for Children, at the City Club the night before. Trim and snappily dressed, she had a stogie in one hand and a glass of cognac in the other. "The understanding is that they come 'sans spouse.' In a lot of cases their wife or girlfriend goes to the Knock Out Abuse benefit, our sister event held on the same night." While the Knock Out Abuse Against Women function explicitly bars men from attending, Fight Night merely caters to male patrons. "It's clearly a men's thing," Contant said. "I'd say they're lightly misbehaving, nothing bad."

Light misbehavior about covers it. Most people connected to Fight Night seemed to consider it a deliciously wicked scene, but, compared to the atmosphere at a typical Saturday night fight card in tank towns across America, gentility prevailed. There were certainly no fistfights in the crowd; no obvious strippers, moonlighting as round-card girls, throwing in a bump-and-grind as they paraded around the ring between rounds; few comments coarser than "Is this a great country or what?" inspired by passing cuties. The patrons were too respectable to risk groping the help at a public charity event, and the hostesses more than competent enough to fend off the few who forgot themselves. Play-acting was the keynote, as patrons and hostesses staged a role-playing fantasy: sugar daddies meet gold diggers.

The greeters shunted arriving guests into party rooms for predinner cocktails, where the hostesses descended on them and turned on the charm. Like a challenger who must take the fight to a defensive-minded champion, the hostesses had the burden of initiating and sustaining the action. They homed in on and broke up male-only conversational clusters, applying a combination of social lubricants to each man. "Hi, I'm Kelli! What's your name? Would you like me to get you another drink? How about a cigar?" It was a massacre. The men knew this attention to be a paid service rather than a product of their own native attractiveness, but they could not help puffing up with pride and good cheer.

They felt like real . . . *guys*. As the cocktail party gathered momentum around him, Joe Robert, the real estate investment mogul and sponsor of the Alexandria Boxing Club who founded Fight Night in 1989, explained that he was originally inspired by an old photograph. "It's a picture I saw in the basement of the Congressional Country Club. There was a label on it that said something like 'Fight Night, 1930' on it, and there's these *guys,* all dressed up, leaning back, with big cigars. It just has this feel, this sense. I was intrigued by it and it stayed with me." Reviving the smoker as a form of nocturnal male socializing, Fight Night 1999 offered men a chance to imagine that they were throwing off several generations' worth of gender training to play, for a few hours, at being the idealized antediluvian *guys* in the picture: robber barons who seize wealth with one hand and dispense it as charity with the other, heroic eaters and drinkers and smokers of unhealthy things, unapologetic oglers of beautiful women, connoisseurs of hitting.

The hired women worked hard to preserve this feeling. The Erickson Agency went all-out to do a first-class job on Fight Night, which had become one of the company's biggest events. Jim Choate, the agency's casting director for television and film, moved through the VIP cocktail party, keeping an eye on his charges at work. Mustached and wearing a long tuxedo coat, he cultivated a nineteenth-century rapscallion look. "We've got about three hundred girls here," he said, "between the greeters, cigar girls, and the hostesses. Thirty handpicked ones, the very best, the most beautiful, are here in the VIP lounge." Choate pointed out this one who had been on television, that one who had been in a print advertisement. "They're here as emissaries, if you will," he continued. "They make the gentlemen comfortable, remind them to have a good time." Tricia Erickson appeared out of the crowd and joined the conversation. "At dinner," she explained, "each of the hostesses on duty will be responsible for a table of ten men. We say, 'Imagine that they're ten little boys and you're the den mother.' Our attitude is that we're motherly and nurturing. We pretend it's a birthday party for all our little boys." Motherhood, not sex, appeared to be the Erickson Agency's preferred rhetoric, although one look around the cocktail party suggested a peculiarly sexy brand of motherhood.

"There's no touching," said Erickson, and Choate emphatically seconded her: "Our girls are told they should not touch, and if anybody touches one of them, she's supposed to tell us and he's out." There appeared to be plenty of social touching going on all around, the kissy routines, hand-on-arm gestures, and shoulder-rubbing that a party entails. And there would be even more of it later, at dinner and after. When a fighter gets tired, his hands come down; when the men had had a few more drinks, their hands began straying to narrow female waists. But there was no ostentatious honking of body parts — what Erickson meant by "touching." Like fight trainers, she and Choate vigilantly monitored the hostesses as they mixed it up with the patrons. "We'll pull a girl aside," Erickson said, "and let her know if we see she's doing something wrong." The hostesses would be on their feet most of the night, with a scheduled break of a few minutes every two hours — long rounds with only brief rests in between.

After cocktails, everyone moved to the International Ballroom for dinner and the show. A laser extravaganza with culminative flash-bang effects filled the room with smoke. Next came the Redskinettes, who had changed into short-shorts, halter tops, and skintight white tubes they wore around their shins above gym shoes, to simulate little white boots. The Pointer Sisters followed, nailing their cues like the pros they were. A hostess standing at ringside unselfconsciously mouthed the words of "I'm So Excited" along with them. The legends of boxing climbed into the ring one by one to be introduced to the crowd by Michael Buffer, the fight announcer who can, as if throwing a switch, fill his voice with genuine-sounding strong feeling. Earnie Shavers, acknowledging applause with a curious two-fingered gesture of benediction, went eighth, before Sugar Ray Leonard and Joe Frazier and after Iran Barkley, Carmen Basilio, Tony DeMarco, Ken Norton, William Joppy, Jake La Motta, and Teofilo Stevenson. They blew kisses, bowed, and mitted the crowd. A couple of the retirees flashed old-time form, dancing and shadowboxing. Frazier punched the air so fiercely that he knocked the boutonniere out of his own lapel while throwing his trademark left hook. He picked the flower off the canvas and put it in his jacket pocket. When all of them had been introduced, the assembled legends formed a line across the ring to receive an ovation, wreathed in smoke still hanging in the air from the laser show.

The evening, having passed in a whirl through concentric circles of make-believe, spiraled closer to its still center: it was time for the hitting. The fights offered few surprises. None of the scheduled mismatches developed into a contest of equals in which the combatants might elicit one another's best work.

The matchmaker, J. D. Brown, a strapping fellow dressed all in black, had explained his task the previous night, at the weigh-in. "Fight Night is a little bit different than other cards," he said, "because the crowd doesn't know that much about the fights. Normally, you just want to match a hometown guy with a win, but here it's a little different. You concentrate on an exciting fight; you don't want two guys who run from each other." This means that displays of technical wizardry do not move the Fight Night crowd, which does most of its fistfight watching at the movies. "Slugger-slugger is a good matchup for this crowd, and slugger-boxer is okay. With a headliner like Camacho, he's defensive, so the other guy's got to come to him." At Fight Night, Brown added, "a fighter's professional decorum matters, too. We don't want any unpleasant surprises for this crowd." That means no ear biting.

The fights were decorous, at least. On the undercard, local up-and-comers honed their craft on tough guys imported for the purpose.

Luther Smith, a welterweight with a 15-0-1 record from Joe Robert's Alexandria Boxing Club, took a six-round decision over a hardy Georgian named Mackie Willis. Smith, a protégé of the local hero Sugar Ray Leonard, moved quickly and well, striking Willis with combinations whenever he wanted to. But he found he couldn't hurt Willis, a solidly built country boy who had augmented hard labor with countless situps and pushups in his garage. Smith's eyes widened when he hit Willis in the body early in the fight and his gloved hand bounced ineffectually off the layers of muscle under the skin. After that, Smith settled for landing pesky slapping blows to the head and then darting away. He won easily because Willis moved so awkwardly, seemingly at cross-purposes with himself, that he robbed his own punches of accuracy and meaningful power.

The other local prospect, a long-bodied welterweight transplant from Guyana named Marlon Haynes, beat a similarly resilient but unthreatening opponent, Dennis Burley, from Scranton, Pennsylvania. Haynes threw hard body punches, but the stockier Burley maintained a defensive posture, gloves high and elbows low, and blocked most of them. Burley made offensive sallies only occasionally and to little effect. He did butt Haynes sharply in the second round, though, scoring a divot under Haynes's right eye that showed up bright pink against the dark skin. Haynes, undeterred, continued to hammer away, adjusting his attack by guiding his punches around Burley's elbows and forearms to his flanks. Burley lasted the four rounds without getting hurt.

In the first headline bout, in which the art of self-defense did not figure prominently, Butterbean knocked out a hirsute, pear-shaped fellow from Cedar Rapids, Iowa, named George Chamberlain. Butterbean, who projected an air of modest good humor, had not let his celebrity as the so-called King of the Four-Rounders go to his head. He knew himself to be a lout and recognized that he owed his improbable renown mostly to his impressive roundness and the hog-calling p.r. efforts of his handlers, a hardbitten crew out of Bay City, Michigan, where heavy hitting and iron-headed valor count for nearly everything. Like a one-man ring version of the Harlem Globetrotters, Butterbean toured the nation besting large but inept men who expected to lose.

Most of Butterbean's fights follow a pattern made semi-inevitable by the class of opponents his managers choose. Typically, Butterbean spends the first round fiercely stamping his front foot and batting his gloves together. If he could roar, he would. He throws a few sweeping punches and people in the crowd exclaim something like, "Whoa, if that one had landed the other guy would be in trouble!"

The opponent gets to hit Butterbean sometime early in the fight, usually not very hard, which is all he can manage. Butterbean smiles at him, sometimes doing a taunting shimmy with his hands held out wide, and the same people exclaim something like, "That didn't hurt him at all! He must have a really thick skull!" Butterbean begins hitting in earnest in the second or third round, often finishing with a knockout. In this case, Chamberlain got into trouble in the third round and made the mistake of turning away, allowing Butterbean to hit him in the kidneys, which always hurts. Butterbean followed with a solid uppercut that finished him. After the fight, Butterbean remained in the ring and climbed out of his trunks. They were auctioned by Michael Buffer for a high bid of $4,500 (made by the president of an airline), the money going to Fight for Children. Under the trunks, Butterbean wore sail-sized underwear with smiley faces on them.

We are tempted to think of boxing as show business. Television money and ratings dictate who, when, and even how the important boxers fight. Most people, especially casual fans who drop in on boxing only for the occasional high-profile television bout, respond to boxers' personas the way they respond to Hollywood stars, as an amalgam of the player and the character played: Tyson the self-detonating time bomb, Ali the people's prince, Holyfield the holy warrior. Matchmaking entails not just an exciting encounter of fighting styles but the crafting of narrative and symbolic resonance that encourages consumer buys: bad boy meets good guy; fallen hero seeks revenge against nemesis; new order meets old school. You can find the pitch compressed into the inane high-concept promotional epithets attached to fight cards: The Battle for Redemption! This Time It's Personal! Look Out Below! (The last of these would have made a good slogan touting the contest between Mike Tyson and the groin-punching Andrew Golota, the era's two most notorious heavyweight foulers.)

Those who regard boxing as mired in a particularly enfeebled present era often claim that it is coming to resemble pro wrestling — similarly scripted to angle for predictable thrills in place of honest combat, similarly eager to treat its audience with contempt. Others regard the boom in pro wrestling, which has long had cable television in a profitable hammerlock, as a warning to boxing to get its marketing act together or suffer total eclipse by the media-savvier imitation blood sport. But pro wrestling, unlike boxing, falls entirely within the ambit of show business. Sometimes at a big multipurpose gym, like Gleason's in Brooklyn, wrestlers will be slinging each other off the ropes and felling each other with titanic-looking blows in one ring while boxers spar in another. You can see the difference in what they are preparing for. The wrestlers rehearse, the way actors do, going over elements of an athletic drama they will play-act in the ring. The boxers, also working at their craft, are not getting ready to play-act. They have to be ready and fit precisely because they don't know what's going to happen when they get in the ring and the hitting starts.

Show business does perform an important function at the fights, though. We want to know that hitting means something, and making it part of a story, a drama, a formulaic scenario, helps it to signify. At Fight Night, for instance, all the hitting is done for a good cause. Show business does not have to be extraneous window-dressing, either; the show-business aspects of a boxing match can affect what happens in the ring. Fighters make stylistic changes to prove to audiences and matchmakers their marketability as knockout artists or their ability to go the distance. Underdogs press harder against notorious headliners because they know that judges, even unbribed ones, tend to look for reasons to award close rounds to celebrity fighters, as if it would be a shame to spoil the story line. And fighters do sometimes pretend in the ring — not just when taking a dive or otherwise faking a fight, but also in honestly contested ones. Ali, more than anyone, play-acted in and out of the ring so habitually that his opponents had trouble figuring out what effect their punches actually had on him. Earnie Shavers knew he had nailed Ali early in their bout in 1977, and he could see that Ali looked hurt, but he hesitated to rush in to exploit the advantage because he suspected that Ali was faking to lure him into a trap. Ali, who later admitted that Shavers had hurt him in several rounds, recovered and won by decision. Ali worked his magic against Shavers, but the logic of hitting was already catching up with him as he slowed down and relied increasingly on gamesmanship and a good chin. Ali had been so fast and confident in his youth that he seemed almost immune to being hit, but by the time he fought Shavers he was taking all that deferred punishment, gesturing heroically to assure the audience that he was fine.

Behind the screen of show business, behind the second screen of sports-talk convention that might fool one into believing that boxing is about winning and losing and competition, behind even the business transactions that shape the trade, the part of boxing where force meets technique remains significantly untouched by theatrical commerce. Boxing may be dramatic, and there are few things more dramatic than a close fight between well-matched equals, but the hitting at its core is the opposite of pretending.

Macho Camacho, the main attraction in Fight Night's other headline bout, did not intend to be upstaged by Butterbean's underwear. As the sound system cranked "Livin' La Vida Loca," he stormed up the aisle to the ring, apparently eager to reveal his getup: an elongated and high-slit white leather loincloth emblazoned with the Puerto Rican flag and topped off with matching cape. Entering the ring with sixty-nine victories and multiple championships on his record, Camacho had the air of a practiced trouper. Some of his concern for entertaining self-presentation proceeded from natural vanity, but some of it was a veteran's shtick: because he did not intend to trade haymakers with his opponent, he made it up to the crowd with antics and decor. That opponent, Manuel Esparza, a calm and unsmiling young fellow, was no slugger, either.

Once Camacho had shed his cape and the bout began, it became clear that both fighters knew what they were doing; it was also clear that Esparza could not win. Esparza gamely found ways to reach Camacho with punches, but the punches did no damage. Early in the fight, he hit Camacho directly on the button with a straight right and nothing happened. Camacho, realizing how easy his task would be, abandoned his usual strategy of feeling out his opponent and stepped in to land solid lefts to the body and the head. Camacho, a southpaw, had never been a terrific puncher, but he could hit hard enough when he wanted to, and in latter years he had shown an inclination to make up for waning handspeed by putting more leverage into power punches. By the fourth round, a mouse had ballooned under Esparza's left eye. Camacho forced him to the ropes and put him down with an uppercut. As the referee tolled over him, Esparza collected himself in a crouch, squeezing every second of recovery from the count before getting up. Rising from the squat by pushing with his gloves against the canvas, he looked like a very tired old man anticipating a hot bath. Camacho belabored him some more before the bell.

Esparza sat heavily in his corner between rounds, hurt, sullen, losing the fight and unequipped to do anything about it. When he left his stool at the bell for the fifth, gloved hands pushing down on his thighs in a repeat of the old man's gesture of rising, he looked drained of force. Camacho, by contrast, seemed to inflate with potency, like a demonic Michelin Man, every time he landed a blow. When the mouse under Esparza's eye opened and he began to bleed, the ring doctor took it as an excuse to stop the fight.

*   *   *

The sight of Earnie Shavers in the ring at Fight Night —
even as a noncombatant, dressed up and taking his bows
— reminded me of a punch he threw twenty-one years before. Maybe the fights that followed helped raise the ghost:
the way Camacho's punches seemed to take the life out of
Esparza, the way Marlon Haynes put the leverage of legs
and shoulders into his body shots, the way Butterbean's
blow to the kidneys made Chamberlain look like an actor
mistakenly run through for real in a stage duel. I could see
a younger Shavers, stripped to his trunks, hitting Larry
Holmes with a thunderous right cross in 1979.

The Holmes-Shavers bouts were textbook encounters
between slugger and boxer. Holmes, like Macho Camacho, is a defensive expert who made a distinguished career
out of not getting hit flush with hard punches. Unlike Camacho, Holmes always looked to denature the other guy's
attack with preemptive punches of his own, turning good
defense into a form of offense. Constantly jabbing from
long range as he moved to stay out of harm's way, Holmes
won a commanding twelve-round decision over Shavers in
1978, then TKO'd Shavers in the eleventh round of the rematch the following year. Holmes won almost every one of
the twenty-two-plus rounds they fought in the two bouts,
but in the one round Holmes definitely did not win — the
seventh of their second fight — Shavers caught him flush.

"I made a mistake," said Holmes on the phone. He, like
other master craftsmen of boxing, makes a policy of re-
membering even the most inspired accomplishments of his
opponents as resulting from his own easily rectified errors;
it is part of regarding what happens in the ring as knowable

and under his control. "I started feeling sympathy for him," said Holmes. "He was bleeding all out his eye, all swelled up, and I started thinking about it. That's when he coldcocked me." Shavers's face did look awful by the seventh round, especially around the eyes. Holmes had been steadily pulping it with his signature variant of the old one-two: a tireless, cumulatively murderous left jab punctuated with a variety of idiosyncratic looping right-hand punches he used at closer range. Holmes, who had a habit of leaving his gloved fist open when he punched, had also probably thumbed Shavers in the eye at least once earlier in the fight. So Shavers was in trouble, but in the seventh he managed to land a punch or two in return, hard shots but not quite flush, and finally got inside Holmes's timing.

Holmes retreated, as he often did to get the spacing right between himself and an advancing opponent, then he made a stand and started a punch on the way. But Shavers, stepping forward in a compact mass, was already into his own move, a right cross thrown as it should be: hips and shoulder turning to produce a short, straight punch just like those he demonstrated in the restaurant of the Hilton. It has been described as a Hail Mary blow, but it had nothing to do with prayer or providence: Shavers, punching by the book, hit Holmes on the jaw in strictly orthodox fashion. Holmes went down with a finality one does not often see, not even in the movies, as sense and life went out of his body all at once. It looked like he had been shot with a tranquilizer dart just as he stepped on a land mine. Collapsing and leaping at the same time, he crashed to the canvas as if from a great height.

Boxers get hit and they fall down; there's nothing extraordinary about that. But boxers hit by Shavers, even those known for their good chins and self-possession, responded with peculiarly exaggerated distress. Holmes was out cold for only a moment as he fell, but in that moment he had the awful stateliness of a spaceship, its crew and mechanical systems wiped out by some hideous force, adrift forever in the cosmos.

Amazingly, Holmes woke up, rolled over, got his wobbly legs under him, and staggered to his feet before the referee could count to ten. He had hit the floor hard enough to knock a man out — or, as he claims now, to bring a man to. "I was completely out for a couple of seconds," said Holmes, "but the pounding I took when I landed on the floor woke me up." Nobody can say what woke him up, but it's important to Holmes, as it is to the Federal Aviation Administration after a mysterious plane crash, that there be recoverable explanations for even the most irrecoverably traumatic events. Shavers went after Holmes to finish him off, but the round was almost over. Unsteady but regaining his wits, Holmes punched and held and made Shavers miss him, managing to last to the bell. One minute on his stool between rounds provided the respite Holmes needed. By the bell for the eighth, he had regained his equilibrium. Still far ahead on points, he returned to his measured style, pasting the half-blind and faltering Shavers without mercy for three more rounds until the referee stopped it in the eleventh.

But Shavers had given Holmes a blow to remember him by. "I will never forget it," Holmes said with a certain pride, and there was a long pause in which we held our respective phones to our ears and considered it once more: for him, the prodigious impact of the punch and then waking up on the deck, the lights gone strange, the hurt taste of rust and bone in his mouth, the crying need to beat the count already urging him to arrange his balky limbs for the enormous task of standing upright; for me, an old videotape in which Shavers pours all of himself into the punch and Holmes's untenanted body is falling. I have never seen a man go down harder in a fight he ended up winning.

Butterbean had held the whole crowd's attention, but as Fight Night proceeded the patrons gradually turned away from the ring. Most of them were deep in conversation by the time Camacho finished with Esparza. Only a hard core of spectators, mostly younger men standing with arms folded, gathered around the ring to watch the remaining undercard fights after the main events. And most of these had given up by the time a Ukrainian named Sergiy Ivashin beat Mike McFail of Baltimore by decision in the four-round nightcap shortly after midnight. The show was over; as show business, it had been over for some time. Now it was just a white guy and a black guy who both weighed about 150 pounds circling in the ring, hitting each other. The patrons were gorged with hitting. After steak and good booze and chocolate desserts in the shape of boxing gloves, after chatting up the babes and getting an eyeful, after shaking hands with Carmen Basilio or Earnie Shavers, after an evening of fights, they'd had enough.

A fighter's appetite and tolerance for hitting is elemental; it comes before the role-playing of fistic show biz, and it must come even before boxing technique. Mastering the craft means fashioning a style that takes maximum advantage of one's root capacity for hitting and minimizes the necessity of taking advantage of one's root capacity for being hit. In the course of his career, Shavers, a single-mindedly offensive fighter who admits that his idea of defense was "throwing my right hand," had plenty of opportunities to find out how much he could take as well as how much he could dish out. But even when he first put on the gloves, even before he began his true education in how to box, he already knew he could hit. "I had power from the beginning," said Shavers. "I knew it. First time I got in a ring in the gym, first time I hit a guy, he flew across the ring. He was a Gold Gloves fighter, a champion, out of Youngstown. It was my first time sparring. I hit him and he flew. Everybody said, 'What was *that?*'" Even after speed and suppleness have abated over the years, the capacity for hitting remains. "Power doesn't go away," he said. "I still have probably seventy-five percent of the power I once had."

Shaking Shavers's hand, slapping him on the back, laying hands on him, the patrons of Fight Night could feel that truth and be satisfied in a way that goes deeper than show biz and into the places where force precedes meaning.

5

Out of Order

I saw the picture of Gary's leg just once, and for only a few seconds. We were walking down Seventh Avenue, a block from Madison Square Garden, on our way to see Lennox Lewis defend his heavyweight titles against Michael Grant on April 29, 2000. I had first met Gary a couple of hours earlier when our fight-going group, assembled by a mutual friend, convened at a Mexican restaurant for dinner and drinks. Before that, I had known Gary as a noted trader of fights on videotape and as the author of some of the few on-line boxing commentaries worth reading. His polite, history-minded epistles, posted to a discussion site dominated by angry free-associaters, stood out from the heaving mass of Internet fight prose on the order of "Hay Jack Ass, NO WAy cud that crybaby Jack Johnson defete Mike Tyson!!! IMO IRon Mike wood kick his ASS just like Im gonna kick your's ass fagett. "

The evening was shaping up, for me and for Gary (who had come to New York for the bout from his home in western Wisconsin), to be one of those in which a friend invites you to join him and some people he knows, but then the friend gets busy with the other people, and you end up thrown together with strangers. On the walk to the Garden, Gary and I fell into step and struck up a conversation about the gradual runup in the size of heavyweights during the twentieth century, which provided a suitable context for the evening's main-event contest between Lewis (6'5", 247 pounds) and Grant (6'7", 250 pounds). We found ourselves agreeing on most points and exchanging choice morsels of esoterica; making friends, in other words. When we came within sight of the Garden, Gary interrupted himself in midsentence: "Hold on, I want to show you something." We stopped walking; the fight-bound crowd pushed by around us. "This is what I'm all about," he said, producing a photograph from his wallet and handing it to me. I was expecting a picture of his children, or his wife, or an obliging ex-champion posed shoulder-to-shoulder with Gary.

It was a snapshot of a mangled leg. Better than I remember the picture itself, I remember the shock of seeing it, and of realizing that Gary carried it around like Saint Lucy carrying her put-out eyes on a tray. I can call up only a general impression of pale skin awash in gore, as if the leg had been drained of its fluids and then basted in them as they clotted, and a quality of torsion in the unnaturally bent limb that made my own bones want to break in sympathy or disgust. I can't remember for certain the color of the hospital bedding, blue or green, on which the leg was laid out. But I can summon up without effort the sensation of my skin tightening all over, going cool, as if I were preparing for a secondary impact even as I recoiled from the force of collision implicit in the picture.

"What the hell happened to *you?*" seemed like the thing to say, although "What if it happens to *me?*" would have been the more heartfelt response, but I passed the photo back to him without comment, nodding to indicate that he should give me the rest of it. A doctor, Gary said, had taken the picture before operating on his leg after a car crash in 1987. The other guy, panicky drunk on the highway, made a mistake and sailed his car over the divider into oncoming traffic, hitting Gary's car head-on and crushing it. The emergency crew took ninety minutes to cut Gary out of the wreckage.

Everything that came after was marked After. Gary married and then divorced, worked as an accountant for a series of companies that went out of business or otherwise failed him, and arrived at a monkish life organized around day-trading stocks from home, training for marathons, and studying the fights he collected on videotape. He had not run in earnest since college, more than a decade before the crash, but, partially recovered from his injuries and limping on a permanently damaged right leg that might give out at any time, he had set himself the goal of qualifying for the Boston Marathon. That was what he was all about now:

running against the clock and his own limitations, timing the market, not having anyone to answer to, paying devout attention to the world and other people's efforts to cope with it, being the guy who had been in the crash and came out better than Before. His interest in boxing took on central importance in this After life. He saw new shades of virtue, fresh purpose, in fighters' reckoning with matters he now knew well: the life-changing effects of hitting, the management of pain and will, the disciplined exercise of technique in a climate of hurt.

From our seats in the first row of a high balcony, which seemed to hang directly above the ring, Gary and I watched Lennox Lewis put his left glove behind Michael Grant's neck, cradling the younger challenger's lowered head with a fatherly gesture, when he delivered the right uppercut that ended the bout in the second round. That sort of holding and hitting is illegal because it greatly increases the force of the blow, removing the other man's capacity to absorb it by recoiling. Grant was asking to be fouled in exactly that way by putting his head down to charge in swinging, like a soused college football star intent on taking a poke at a bouncer, but it was still a foul. Not that the outcome of the fight was in doubt by then. Grant had already been floored repeatedly by Lewis, who awaited his rushes and punched judiciously, calm as ever — a studied calm that trickles into the cracks in his opponents' psyches, then freezes and expands, encouraging them to fall apart.

After the fights, Gary and I walked up from the Garden to Jimmy's Corner, a long, narrow fight bar on 44th Street just off Times Square. Lewis fans from England jammed the place, part of the black-T-shirted, fight-song-bellowing regiment that had flown into New York to cheer on their champion. They lorded it over anybody who would listen to them. One three-sheeted gent, who alternately slumped over his beer at the bar and rushed about buttonholing strangers in a triumphal fury, called out to nobody and everybody, "Yew facking Americans! We beat you good this time!"

If Lewis's defeat of a physically impressive but untried challenger like Grant was no big deal, really, I could forgive the British fans for celebrating as if it were. They had been unmoored from their senses by the reverberations of a blow to their nation's boxing pride, first felt in the late nineteenth century when the United States supplanted Great Britain as the fight world's dominant power, that is renewed with special force each time a British heavyweight contender slams melodramatically to the canvas. When Lewis, an Englishman of Jamaican parentage, won the WBC belt in 1993, he became the first generally acknowledged British heavyweight titleholder since the spindly-legged, freckled genius Bob Fitzsimmons, who took the title from one American in 1897 and lost it to another in 1899. Fitzsimmons's defeat inaugurated a one-sided series of transatlantic drubbings in the fight world's premier division that spanned most of the twentieth century. Picture Rocky Marciano pulping Don Cockell, memorably described by A. J. Liebling as "a fat man whose gift for public suffering has enlisted the sympathy of a sentimental people"; Muhammad Ali drumming on Brian London's prominent jaw, which even those disposed to avoid using the usual words for the usual things must describe with reference to a lantern; Mike Tyson leaping up through Frank Bruno's metronomic defense to administer giant-killing shots to the head. (A year after defeating Grant, Lewis himself would fall into line, arms flung over his head to create about nine feet of laid-out British heavyweight, when a guy from Baltimore named Hasim Rahman starched him with an overhand right. For British fight fans, it would be a familiar trauma.)

Sometime in the early morning, Gary decided to walk down to Penn Station to catch a late train out to Long Island, where he was staying with our mutual friend. He made his way out of Jimmy's Corner, limping noticeably on his stiff right leg after a long day in which he had climbed and descended many stairs. In his boxy feed cap, gaunt and modest in a particularly upper-midwestern way, he moved among the watchful New York fight people and the shouting, flushed Englishmen who were buying beers five at a time to beat last call.

If you go to the fights, or get in fights, or if you have ever been in a car wreck, you may have noticed that hitting alters perception. Absorbing a hard shot, whether as recipient or spectator, can make you feel as if you were dreaming, or moving in slow motion, shrouded in fog or suddenly liberated from it for the first time in your life by a miraculous gust of wind. Some people, including fighters trying to get up in time to beat the count, find themselves engrossed by a seemingly trivial detail, like a cornerman's odd expression or the texture of a bystander's shirt. In my case, hitting makes things seem to happen out of order.

I heard sound backward, effect before cause, when I got broadsided at the intersection of Humphrey and Orange in New Haven on a rainy weekday morning in 1991. I heard — I hear — breaking glass before the crunch of metal on metal, both before the screech of ineffectual braking, all the sounds of the collision well before the shock of it. In the moment before the crash I made a crazy open-mouthed face and heaved the wheel decisively to one side. I also realized with a curious air of disinterest that I should step on the gas rather than the brakes; if I slowed down, the prow of the fast-closing Buick Park Avenue would strike my smaller and more easily crushed car directly on the driver's side door and end up in my lap. But it was only after the impact, when my car was tilted up on its two right-side wheels and skidding sideways across the rain-slick intersection with the other car wedged into it just back of my driver's side door and pushing like a snowplow, that I silently asked myself, "Why is that car coming at me so fast?"

My car finally separated from the Buick, slammed back down, its tires squealing briefly on the wet pavement, and came to rest. It was nosed downward at a precarious slant with its front wheels dangling free, halfway into a sort of open grave thoughtfully prepared for it by the water authority, which had for several weeks been doing something mysterious to underground pipes in that part of town. The front of my car just missed a guy working in the hole. He was bent over, probably digging, and thereby avoided a slapstick beheading by inches when I crashed in from above to join him. He popped up at the end of my hood, a blocky young man gone O-mouthed in surprise but already shifting from panic to rage, and began scrabbling over the car to get at me. I pointed over my shoulder and said, "His fault. He ran the red." I didn't shout, and my window was rolled up and unbroken, but I enunciated precisely to facilitate lip reading. The guy nodded briskly, climbed off the hood, and exited the hole by another route, now intent on confronting the other driver. Somebody was going to have to suffer for scaring him so badly. Then I thought, for the first time, "Uh-oh, looks like there's going to be an accident," and began worrying that my daily routine might be interrupted.

My car was totaled (the Buick was not), I ended up in the emergency room (the Buick's occupants were fine), and I had a stiff back for years afterward, but it was not one of those cataclysmic high-speed collisions like Gary's that turn machines and bodies into horribly progressive art. Neither car could have been going more than thirty or thirty-five miles per hour. A cop did write me a warning for traveling too fast for conditions — which, as I pointed out to him while the ambulance crew prepared to take me away and the wreckers loaded my stove-in car onto a flatbed truck, did not mean much when the most pertinent condition was another car running a red light at the same speed and crashing into me. In fact, I would not have been crashed into at all had I been going even faster, or, for that matter, driving backward on the sidewalk. The cop maintained an air of august indifference to such hairsplitting.

Our minds process a blow by rearranging their contents around it until the revised whole makes some kind of workable sense. My out-of-order experience of a hard shot (and other people's movielike or dreamlike sensation) is really the initial stage of this mental reordering, the full extent of which depends on the force and timing of the blow, the mind's readiness to absorb it, and the nature of whatever was already taking up space in that mind before the blow landed. If a battle-scarred hell-raiser gets whacked in the eye during his fiftieth barroom melee, his existing apparatus for processing the punch's import will probably be equal to the task. But if I am sucker-punched by a gentle Wordsworth scholar in the English Department's Xerox room, say, or if my wife dry-gulches me with a frying pan for no apparent reason, even a glancing blow would probably oblige me to revise my sense of the world and my place in it. The same goes, to take the point to its grim extreme, for the shock of planes crashing into buildings and the ground on September 11, 2001, a four-blow combination that inspired a lot of people to significantly revise their sense of the world and their place in it. Whether you are trying to figure out the lesson of a boxing match or determine how malign the universe might actually be, the scrambling of perception in the initial experience of the blow cues the scramble to meaningfully rearrange the scattered pieces. It makes sense to me that Gary, processing a shock that changed the course of his life, has committed himself so deeply to collecting and parsing fights. His video library of more than twenty thousand bouts — indexed on cards noting each one's salient features and augmented by a comparable collection of fight books and magazines — amounts to an exhaustive catalogue of hard shots given and taken, reckoned with and succumbed to. Absorbing a decisive punch shapes not only a fight and your experience of it but also the way the fight lives in your head, where you can return to it and make use of it as equipment for living.

That may explain why, when I think back on my car crash, I now find it filed together in memory with two moments — each featuring a big punch — that I have retained in acute detail from an otherwise mostly forgotten evening of Pennsylvania Golden Gloves bouts, held in a nightclub in Erie, that I attended six years later, in 1997.

The first moment occurred in a heavyweight bout between Mike Marzano, from Pittsburgh, and a guy named Shaeffer, from Butler. Marzano, the more skilled boxer and the stronger man, won the first round, jabbing well at long range and moving in to deliver a compact uppercut that snapped back Shaeffer's head. Shaeffer did land a couple of right-hand leads in return, but he had to shift his balance and open his guard too generously in order to throw them. Marzano went back to his corner with the look of a man who had figured out what to do next. In the second round they went back and forth a bit, with Marzano jabbing and Shaeffer's face turning a dark, spoiled shade of red. Then

Shaeffer, who was having no success at hitting Marzano in this round and had probably begun to think about how good it had felt to land those punches in the first, performed the little sideways shift he used to set up a right lead.

Marzano had been waiting for it and responded with programmatic certitude. He turned his shoulder and threw a big, thwacking uppercut to the chin that caught Shaeffer in midmaneuver, still concentrating on unshipping his right hand to punch with it. Shaeffer flew back as if dynamited and landed on forearms and knees, in which position, forehead to the canvas and hindquarters raised as if making obeisance, he was counted out. Marzano, exultant or bemused, froze for the briefest moment in the pose produced by his follow-through — a sweeping line of ridged muscle rising from legs to torso and out along his curved arm to the gloved fist he presented to the nightclub's low, smoke-wreathed ceiling. Towering above his falling opponent, helmeted in the amateur's headgear, Marzano looked like Conan the Barbarian swatting off a Pict's head with a broadax in one of those Frank Frazetta paintings that pervaded the head-shop, automotive, and album-cover stratum of the art world in the 1970s.

Shaken loose from chronology by the decisive one-punch finish, the elements of the event busily rearranged themselves as they occurred. It seemed to me that the inevitable KO had happened long before Marzano actually hit Shaeffer, that Shaeffer's cornermen had already climbed into the ring and were gently removing their downed fighter's headgear when Marzano struck his van-art pose, that the fighters had already left the ring — one with the serene good cheer of a man who has done his job well, the other bracketed by concerned handlers and carefully putting each foot where it belonged while trying not to throw up — when Shaeffer decided it would be a fine idea to try once more that ill-advised move he had used in round one. I can call up in my mind's eye a clear, if completely fanciful, image of Marzano holding his pose, rocklike under the ring lights long after the last bell, while the crowd filed out and the cleanup crew set to work bagging drifts of plastic beer cups and cigarette butts. I remember him already in the pose when I walked in the door and made my way to my seat; I remember him already throwing the uppercut when I was hours away on the interstate, driving to Erie in blowing snow and hoping to get there in time for the first bout.

I can see Marzano throwing the uppercut in a perpetual present tense. He is throwing it right now, and Shaeffer, having allowed himself a lapse in defensive concentration, is about to get flattened. The force of the blow is about to rearrange everything, especially the magnitude of Shaeffer's mistake, around itself. I also clearly remember seeing a green light — I can see it now, and it's green — as I approached the intersection on that rainy morning in New Haven, but occasionally I wonder. Driving through an intersection in my own neighborhood, a familiar routine I had performed hundreds of times before without bad consequences, I allowed myself a lapse in defensive concentration, and the world made me pay for it. Had the guy from the water authority working in the hole straightened up a moment earlier and been killed by my car, I would still be paying for that mistake, now and forever. As it was, I got off easy with a reminder to heed one of the fistic commandments: Protect yourself at all times.

The other punch I remember best from that evening in Erie, now filed with could-have-been versions of my car crash, was a clean miss during the second round of a bout at 139 pounds between Lou Bizzarro Jr. and Jose Otero. Bizzarro had won the first round with crisp counter-punching, meeting and foiling Otero's charges with expert combinations, but in the second he was punching less and devoting more energy to protecting himself. The shorter, more compact Otero had stepped up his efforts to bull Bizzarro into the ropes and maul him there. They had reached that rough halfway point in an amateur fight when a technically proficient young boxer like Bizzarro, hounded by a relentless advancer like Otero, can run out of ideas and throw away his early advantage by giving in to his opponent's insistence on a shot at him. A boxer under constant pressure can become peevish and depressed when navigating the trough between his initial burst of energy and the moment when he finds a working rhythm that can take him through a whole fight. A boxer in that trough, even one who knows better and has trained hard, will sometimes stop moving and bow his head before the approaching storm of punches, as if to say, "What do I have to do to please you? Hit me, then, but please stop following me around." He bends to circumstances, the principal circumstances in this case being his opponent's unwavering desire to hit him and the waning of his own early adrenaline surge. Sometimes both fighters seem to agree that one of them knows better what he wants and that he deserves to get it.

In the second round, Bizzarro found himself in the trough. He had won the first round but he was losing the initiative. Otero, a seasoned amateur, was coming on. They broke for a moment, but Otero immediately closed again, feeling his own growing sense of command and Bizzarro's increasing discomfort. As Otero advanced, though, bulking his shoulders and driving with his legs in expectation of an imminent clash of bodies that would push Bizzarro back to the ropes, Bizzarro got his timing just right and jabbed Otero high on the forehead. It was not a hard enough punch to hurt Otero or dissuade him from advancing, but it perfectly anticipated the murderous overhand right he was getting ready to throw as he rushed in. The jab straightened up Otero a bit, raising him out of his crouch and causing his overhand right to loop a bit higher than he had intended — toward Bizzarro's eyes rather than his chin.

Bizzarro followed the jab with an elegant escape. He shuffled his feet to shift his balance, ducked very low, and sprang under Otero's punch, under his armpit, and past him, untouched. Otero went into the ropes hard, flailing his arm over the top strand, almost throwing himself out of the ring with the force of his suddenly unchecked charge. By the time Otero got himself untangled and turned around, Bizzarro had set himself up in the middle of the ring and the fight had entered its endgame. By doing something exactly right, the way he did it all the time in the gym with his teachers, Bizzarro regained his sense of command. Steadier now, he had made it through the trough and into a fighting groove he could sustain the rest of the way. Otero didn't land any more punches that mattered; Bizzarro won by decision.

Had Bizzarro botched that preemptive jab-and-escape routine, had Otero therefore landed his overhand right to the chin and bounced Bizzarro off the ropes and onto the canvas in a watery-limbed heap, the elements of the sequence would have staged their usual game of musical chairs in my head. The harder and better timed the blow, the more violently it asserts itself upon the order of things. But the more masterly the defensive maneuver that makes a hard punch miss, the more acutely I remember it as a different but equally powerful sort of assertion: it robs the transformative force from a blow that would have made everything strange and new.

Had I somehow caused that Buick to miss me, had I seen it coming and done something inspired involving drastic acceleration and a palming twist of the wheel just so, that would be one kind of memory. I would say: It was a rainy morning, I saw this car, I did this and then that and then one other thing that I once saw somebody do in a similar situation, and the Buick missed me by so little that I could see the blue veins on the underside of the other driver's tongue as we both made crazy open-mouthed faces. I would say: It was on my mind all week, the near miss and a sudden appreciation of the precariousness of the gentle graduate student's life I had in New Haven, an instance of the world's will to strangeness and its (or my) limited but occasionally effective powers of imposing order without doing harm. But the Buick did not miss me, and instead I have a hitting memory, which means breaking glass, paramedics putting tape across my forehead to fix me to a stretcher while asking me if I was sure my head hadn't hit the steering wheel, and a couple of weeks of taking strong muscle relaxants that encouraged me to sit around wondering when what was in my head would unscramble and lose the aura of fatefulness. It happened more than a decade ago, but I can still see the traffic light in my mind's eye — how it sits above the intersection against the backdrop of a slate-gray Connecticut overcast — and it's green. Red. Green.

I wonder how Shaeffer remembers the second round of his fight with Marzano, and if he learned not to lead with his right, or at least not to indulge himself in that telltale sideways shift just before he did. I wonder if Bizzarro, who has since turned pro, ever thinks about the punches he did not get hit with. Probably not. They probably fly past and disappear, since he has a present or future fight on which to concentrate and the punches with which he did get hit to consider.

A single transformative blow knocked Gary into the After portion of his life on Sunday, December 20, 1987. He was

living just outside St. Paul then. He had spent the previous
two days upstate, visiting an old friend whose wife had just
walked out on him and the kids. He and the friend had
been working on an emergency financial plan, and Gary
had also given him a sizable gift of cash to tide him over.
Driving back toward St. Paul, eastbound on I-694, Gary
felt strong, clear, purposeful. The roads were dry as he approached the city at dusk. He looked at his watch — it was
4:47 — and he was thinking he would be home by 5:15, in
time for supper with his girlfriend. "My next three memo-
ries," he wrote to me in an e-mail, "are: (1) lights up in the
distance that seemed separate and distinct from the stream
of car-lights going west, (2) a bronze flash in front of my
car, (3) a bunch of guys crawling all over my car while
smoke and/or steam swirled around in a kind of slow-motion, surreal haze. I remember coming to, being slumped
over, observing the broken windshield, the smoke/steam,
guys crawling all over, the slow-motion feel to the whole
scene and thinking 'Shit, I think I got hit.'"

The guy who hit him, James Haverinen, had been drinking with a female companion that afternoon. Traveling
westbound, he had sideswiped a car on the highway,
which apparently caused him to panic. He began weaving
through traffic at high speed to escape the scene of the first
accident. He lost control of his car while passing on the inner shoulder, closest to the eastbound lanes, and it became
airborne, turning sideways as it crossed the median at an
angle. Entering oncoming eastbound traffic rear end first,
Haverinen's car sheared along the side of a station wagon

and landed squarely on the hood of Gary's car, then bounced into the air again, continuing across the rest of the highway until it hit the guardrail and spun into the ditch next to the eastbound lanes' outer shoulder. "My car," Gary wrote, "at a cruising speed of 60 mph, was stopped COLD, thrown back one car length, and then jack-knifed about 90 degrees into the ditch on the left (median) side." The *Star Tribune* ran a picture of the crash scene the next day. In it, Gary's car looks like a go-cart, just a driver's seat mounted on the naked chassis, the rest having been stripped away in the crash and subsequent efforts to cut him free of the wreckage.

Haverinen, who was thirty-three, Gary's age at the time, was killed. Everybody else — Gary, four people in the station wagon, and Haverinen's companion — got hurt but lived. Gary told me more about the accident at Jimmy's Corner after the Lewis-Grant fight, he encouraged me in our subsequent e-mail correspondence to ask about it, and he wrote a couple of long e-mails in response when I did, but he ignored my queries about the drunk driver's fate. Since Gary is a good correspondent, diligent and thorough, I took his refusal to dwell on the person at fault as a matter of principle on his part, and stopped asking. But I had to know the answer, and for some reason I had to know the guy's name, so I went to the library's microfilm room and found out for myself.

In the days after the accident, Gary made his way through a twilight of surgeries, postsurgical misery, and painkiller-induced visions. Lying in his hospital bed, he stared hard at the ceiling, because whenever he relaxed his attention the ceiling began to move like sand blowing in the desert. When he slept, he dreamed of fighting with a malign world: "I was walking into a room (something seemingly non-threatening, like a home office), and as soon as I would take a step forward, the nearest inanimate [object] (a lamp, a phone) would jump at me. I would recoil, fend it off with my arms, take another step or two forward, and the next object would do the same. I would keep flailing away to defend myself until I would jerk myself awake, in a total sweat . . . I would then lay there calmly, and within 5 or 10 minutes, I would fall asleep, and almost immediately, THE SAME EXACT SEQUENCE would start again . . . This would happen ALL NIGHT LONG."

He left the hospital eleven days after the crash, on New Year's Eve, 1987. In time, patched up and recovering, he emerged from twilight into a new life that had produced his current routine of day-trading, training passionately to bring down his marathon times to the level required to qualify for Boston, and collecting fight tapes. The impact of metal on flesh, rearranging his bones and his priorities, had imbued the details of this routine with a novel quality of fullness and proportion. Running competitively against himself and trying to beat the market offered ways to extract measurable value from every elapsed second of the bonus time he had gained by surviving the crash. Undertaking to archive and master the whole sweep of boxing history gave him a way to turn the shock of hitting into the stuff of coherent narratives, lessons, models. If his mind has mercifully wiped out his experience of the moment when Haverinen's car hit him, Gary can study that blow's countless glove-masked antecedents and echoes.

He does not torture himself by asking what his life would be like if he had not gone to see his friend in trouble, if he had happened to change lanes or performed an amazing action-movie escape just in time for Haverinen's flying car to miss him. He says, rather, that he regrets nothing about the crash, and wouldn't choose to relive his life without enduring it. "I'm a stronger person because of it," he says — more disciplined, more confident, more patient, less governed by fear and thus more open to possibility. When tempted to "start pissing and moaning about current events in my life (getting blown out of three jobs, the divorce, etc)," he restores his sense of the order of things with a look at the picture of his leg.

The After Gary, limping but austerely joyful, takes in stride what might well have made the Before Gary frantic with anger. The crash, he wrote, "opened my eyes a lot about what I like to call the 'ultimate universe,' as distinct from my 'personal universe,' and by so doing, made the latter that much wider and richer and deeper in the long run. I had always been about half-way to where I wanted to be in terms of reconciling and balancing the 'personal' and the 'ultimate'" — by which he means, I think, the real and the ideal — "and this got me quite a bit further down the road (I almost wrote 'the rest of the way,' but there's always room for improvement on this front, IMO . . .)."

Gary counts on there being room for improvement — in

his ability to reconcile the real and ideal, in his running times, and in boxing, too. At first, I was surprised to learn that one major part of his study of the fights is a crusading inquiry into fixes, fakes, and covered-up mismatches. I had thought the After Gary would be the sort of fellow who takes the corruption of boxing, like everything else, as it comes. But his obsessive detective work makes perfect sense — not because he feels himself to have been cheated by James Haverinen or by life, but because fight-tampering prevents boxing from being a pure expression of craft and will rising above circumstance and human limitations. The personal universes of thieving profiteers, weak-souled fighters, and gullible audiences are constantly impinging upon the path to the ultimate universe — the ideal state in which character and technique redeem raw hitting — that should be opened by honest boxing.

So Gary roots out unworthy fights, mostly for his own edification and that of his correspondents. A fix occurs when noncombatants (judges, the referee, the boxing commission, the ring doctor, cornermen) conspire to alter the outcome of a fight honestly contested by the boxers. Usually, one can expect to find people with money and power behind the fix, rewarding participants for their dishonesty. If the judges give the victory to the wrong guy because they are stupid, biased, or benighted in their understanding of boxing style, that's just a bad decision; if they expect to benefit from the bad decision, that makes it a fix. A fake occurs when one or both of the fighters in the ring collude with other profit-motivated parties, tacitly or explicitly, to dictate the outcome of the fight — a category that embraces outright dives and intentionally halfhearted efforts.

Gary accepts that much fixing and faking is tacit — there may not actually be handshakes in back alleys and transfers of cash-filled sacks — but he is still a conspiracy theorist. A boring heavyweight title fight like the first one between Lennox Lewis and Evander Holyfield, which ended in a hotly debated draw, will whip Gary into a speculative lather. Did the fight's inconclusiveness proceed from more than just a failure of styles to mesh? Did one (or both) stay away from the other (or each other) on purpose to guarantee a big-money rematch at low risk? Were the judges fixed? Was it a fake *and* a fix? He is just as driven to poke holes in the apparently smooth surface of an obscure fight. When a former contender making a comeback scored two consecutive knockouts in which he punched a hapless opponent through the ropes, Gary studied the episodes on tape and reported his dark suspicion that at least the second *SportsCenter*-worthy KO was staged, perhaps as part of a plot to position the former contender for one last title shot.

History, too, is not safe from Gary's critical scrutiny. Why, for instance, is there so little film available of the young Rocky Marciano's fights? What evidence of systematic mismatching, fixing, and faking do certain shadowy conspirators want to prevent us from seeing? Could much of Marciano's career have been a setup job? If so, the legendary diligence and resilience of Marciano become at least in part theater-for-profit, rather than virtue, and we can no longer continue to rank him high on the all-time list of heavyweights. Even in the absence of proof that any of Marciano's fights were crooked, Gary thinks he should rank lower because he didn't fight enough first-rate opponents. Gary does not have any special animus toward Marciano, but it bothers him that Marciano may be getting credit for rising to the challenge posed by a more difficult set of opponents and conditions than he actually faced.

Just after the new year in 2002, I received in the mail from Gary a small envelope containing a single densely printed sheet of paper in tiny type, folded neatly in thirds and then folded again in two, on which all of Marciano's opponents were listed in order, with comments next to each indicating why Marciano's victory over him should be taken with a grain of salt. Harold Mitchell had not won any of his twelve bouts and had been inactive for six months when he fought Marciano, Red Applegate had lost eleven of his twelve most recent bouts, Don Mogard had lost seven consecutive bouts, and so on for every one of Marciano's forty-nine victories. The cuts suffered by Marciano in his two fights with Ezzard Charles are widely reputed to be among the worst ever inflicted in the ring, a brow gashed clear to the bone and a nose torn half off, but Gary wants to see close-up pictures before he believes any of that — and he finds it potentially sinister that he hasn't come across one yet.

The quality of a fight person's suspicions can say much about what he gets out of boxing. Gary distrusts what he sees; I distrust what I read. I'm not as worried as he is about fixes and fakes, and he's more willing than I am to take writers (including boxer-memoirists) at their word as to what happened and why. I am suspicious of fight prose, including my own. The further a writer goes beyond simply recording the tale of the tape and the official result, the more that writer imposes form on a fight by trying to find words to describe it. I know that a single punch landed in a ring five feet or five thousand miles away from me can reorder my experience of a fight and of everything linked to it in my head, and I know this effect inevitably guides my attempt to render the event in writing. I count on such guidance, in fact, since without it I can only list the Fight Fax information and perhaps offer verbatim transcripts of interviews with the participants. So I am inclined not to read fight writing primarily as an account of what happened. I read it, gladly, as an expression of what a fight or a fighter means to the writer.

Gary, on the other hand, is not inclined to trust the fight itself as a full and fair expression of the fighters' combatant selves. He sees their transcendent progress from their constrained personal universes toward the ultimate universe blocked by circumstance and their own weakness, and he feels for them even as he sternly judges their failures. No matter how much dirt he turns up, though, he does not give up on boxers or on boxing. The next blow could change everything. He learned the hard way that a cataclysmic impact can sometimes reopen a blocked path. I am perhaps one life-changing shot away from knowing the truth of that hard lesson in my very bones.

6

The Switch

KEVIN KELLEY, the Flushing Flash, a veteran feather-weight out of New York City noted for having plenty of heart and a high-action fighting style, was in trouble. His right eye, swollen shut, bulged so drastically above and below the sealed eyelashes that it resembled some kind of meat custard with a black rubber band pulled tight around it. His opponent, Derrick "Smoke" Gainer, had damaged the eye in the fourth round — by thumbing, claimed Kelley and his corner, rather than with a clean punch, not that the referee or anyone else cared. Gainer had been pounding the eye since then, each blow inflating it a little more and filling Kelley's head with forked lightning. Effectively blind on that side, Kelley was getting hit with punches he couldn't see coming. The ring doctor, who visited Kelley's corner after the seventh round to inspect the eye, let him continue for the moment, but he would stop the fight soon if Gainer kept hitting it. Eye swelling had cost Kelley his WBC title eighteen months earlier, the first loss of his career after forty-one consecutive victories. Since that defeat, he had won two bouts but also had two draws. Two weeks short of his twenty-ninth birthday, he was in danger of sliding from top-of-the-line featherweight to high-end trial horse. Kelley came out for the eighth round knowing that he was in deep trouble and time was short.

It had been, to that point, not only a stirring entertainment but also a good boxing match. Gainer, who was stepping up in class of opposition, was faster, taller, and younger. Kelley, who held the semi-meaningless World Boxing Union title (as opposed to the much more prestigious, and thus at least semi-meaningful, WBC title he had once held), was far more ring-wise, and he hit harder. In the contest of styles, Gainer tried to keep Kelley at arm's length, while Kelley, the better infighter and body puncher, tried to close the range. The fighters, both of whom were left-handed, had traded knockdowns in the third round (although the referee called one a slip). Kelley had gone down in the fourth when his eye got hurt, but he had come out for the fifth, the eye already useless, and dropped Gainer with an overhand left. "Look what you did with one eye," said Phil Borgia, Kelley's trainer, when his fighter came back to the corner after the fifth. In the sixth, seventh, and eighth, however, Gainer exploited the advantage that Kelley's injury had given him. Gainer moved in closer and sat down on his punches, as they say, which means planting oneself long enough to put authority into a blow rather than flicking it at long range and moving briskly out of harm's way. As Kelley took head shots on his vulnerable right side and the eye got worse, spectators and ringside officials began coming around to the doctor's view that somebody would soon have to save him from himself. George Foreman, working the broadcast for HBO, said it might be time to stop the fight.

In Kelley's corner, the great cutman Al Gavin had been doing what he could to limit the swelling, and Borgia had been trying to make his fighter stick to the plan. Borgia wanted Kelley to jab and then step in behind the jab to work up close to Gainer, where he could do damage while protected from Gainer's long punches. When a fighter with confidence in his punching power gets hurt, though, he will often abandon his trainer's plan, instead throwing haymakers as he seeks salvation with a quick knockout. When he does that, he opens himself to taking more punches and hastens his own defeat. Borgia had to stop Kelley from falling into that error.

After the fourth, when Kelley came back to the corner with his eye freshly hurt and closing, Borgia had made a little speech that followed his usual rhetorical pattern: get the fighter's attention, state a philosophical principle, suggest an application of that principle, and equip the fighter with a mantra for the following round, repeating where necessary. "Look at me," Borgia said. "Look at me. *Look. At. Me.* You trained to fight with no eyes or not? Look at me!

We are trained to fight with no goddamn eyes. You got that?" Kelley, who was sitting on his stool and looking at Borgia with his good eye, the left one, said, "I got it." Borgia went on: "You got one eye. That means you got to work that right even more on the switch. You got me?" He gave Kelley some water from a bottle. "It don't mean a thing, Kev. Remember what our motto is: It don't mean a thing." Borgia, who has a lot of mottoes, was reminding his fighter that an ecstatic insistence on the fight plan would transcend injury and other contingencies, and he was modifying the plan in one particular: Kelley could protect his right eye by switching to a right-handed stance from time to time, in which the left eye leads and the right is sheltered.

Switching from lefty to righty stances had always been part of Kelley's repertoire. Borgia teaches his fighters to do everything from both stances, just in case. But he had in mind more than just a defensive adjustment. He *knew* — in the way that a true believer knows, but also in the way that a technician knows — that Kelley could knock Gainer out by switching from lefty to righty stances while on the attack, a potent but risky move that Borgia sometimes calls a turnover. When Kelley timed a turnover just right, as he had when he had dramatically knocked out Jose Vida Ramos with the move two years earlier, he seemed to materialize suddenly in front of his opponent with a terrific left-handed punch already on the way, having miraculously passed through the other man's field of fire by taking a shortcut through a neighboring dimension. Just before the bell for the sixth round, Borgia put his lips close to Kelley's ear. "And work your turnovers," he said. "He's *there* when you're on the inside." His voice had the passionate rasp of conviction: get inside, switch, and you can still win this fight.

Three rounds later, in the eighth, Gainer was deep into his rhythm, leaning into his punches with the abandon of a formerly skittish young boxer well on the way to making his fortune by knocking out a champion. He stepped in and threw a left; as he did so, he dropped his right hand, a bad habit. Kelley had anticipated the left and was already into his move. To switch on the fly from lefty to righty, throwing his own punch while avoiding Gainer's, Kelley had to do four things at the same time: he brought his trailing foot, the left, forward in advance of the right so that it became his lead foot; he turned his trunk so that his left shoulder became his lead shoulder; he craned his head and torso far to the right to allow Gainer's punch to pass harmlessly overhead; and he threw a chopping overhand left that started as sort of a cross thrown from a left-handed stance but, as he moved his feet and turned his trunk and shoulders, became more of a hook thrown from a right-handed stance. With his entire self in concentrated motion behind the punch, Kelley hit Gainer right on the button.

Gainer folded up and went down as if he had been preset, like a light on a timer, to lose consciousness a moment before Kelley's punch landed. He rolled over onto his back after he hit the canvas and lay there, quivering. The referee counted to seven before waving his hands to indicate that Gainer was finished. The ring filled up instantly, as it always does at the end of a big fight, with officials, functionaries, members of the fighters' factions, television people, and other credentialed noncombatants eager to get through the ropes. Most of them milled around in unconvincing mimicry of purposeful behavior. Gainer remained down but alert as his cornermen and the doctor, crouching amid all the legs coming and going, worked on him while safeguarding him from being trampled. Meanwhile, Kelley climbed onto the ropes in his corner, shouting and making exultant gestures with his gloved hands at the crowd in the arena and all the people in front of their televisions, wherever they were. Borgia, smiling behind his fierce little beard and mustache, helped Kelley keep his balance. The victor's nose was bleeding, and there was blood on his face. His eye looked worse than ever, alien and archaic, as if afflicted by a condition for which there had not been a name since the Middle Ages. But he had proven that he was still a featherweight to be reckoned with. This was in June 1996.

The fight world tells itself stories to make swollen-shut eyes and quivering supine bodies mean something to fans, reporters, and maybe even fighters. Until Kelley saved the Gainer bout with a one-punch knockout, the latter portion of his career had conformed to the familiar tale of a ring-worn former world-beater whose prospects diminished along with his speed and resilience. When Gainer went down and stayed down, though, Kelley became a resurgent former world-beater, still tough and perhaps more dangerous than ever because he learned from experience.

Kelley, who won his next three fights as well, therefore became the perfect opponent for Prince Naseem Hamed, a rising young Yorkshireman of Yemeni parentage who had run up an undefeated record against undistinguished competition. A left-hander who switched promiscuously among southpaw, right-handed, and less identifiable stances, Hamed had made a name for himself with a line of shameless big talk and a wild-looking, rubbery-bodied fighting style that regularly produced knockouts. Those crowd-pleasing KO's were understood to validate the shabbier elements of his showmanship: the vaguely embarrassing dance he performed during his ring walks, like a miniature Chippendale trained in European discos; the will-he-or-won't-he buildup before he performed the front flip over the ropes with which he entered the ring; the postfight rhapsodies about the wonderfully marketable power with which Allah had infused him, the incomparable Naz. He backed up all the preening, people said, by flattening opponents, and that was the key to his success in making the difficult crossing from fighter to entertainer. Hamed was a celebrity, at least in Great Britain and the Middle East.

But Americans (who were unlikely to embrace an Arab star even before September 11, 2001) took little notice of the Prince except as a curiosity: a bat-eared foreign popinjay whose yo-dog-yo dialogue came wrapped in an English accent and whose parodically "American" boxing style often collapsed from improvisational looseness into slapstick. In order to breach the American television-and-publicity complex, where the real money and fame could be had, Hamed had to win a high-profile bout in the United

States against a leading featherweight. Kelley was American, which helped, and by knocking Gainer out he had refreshed his image as a battle-hardened campaigner with serious horseshoes in his gloves. He was just ring-worn enough to give Hamed confidence that youthful energy would overwhelm experience, but plenty of people accepted the version of the Kelley story that said he was not yet over the hill. Also, he was popular in New York, which would help fill Madison Square Garden and give the television announcers another element to weave into their story lines when he fought Hamed: local hero makes last stand against brash young Ali-in-the-making.

Hamed's unorthodox style, combined with speed and unlikely power, would present Kelley with a difficult problem. In most fights, the combatants tacitly agree on how they will conduct themselves. "We will fight like this," they determine by fistic telepathy in the early rounds. "X will lead, and Y will counterpunch; X will trap Y in the corners, but Y will decide when we clinch," and so on. The fighter who succeeds in imposing terms advantageous to him usually wins, but even in an unequal contest the two combatants usually arrive at a working arrangement by some sort of compromise, around which the fight takes form. The referee, when he knows his business, enforces the terms of the fighters' compromise. Hamed refuses to fight that way. Instead of making a deal, he invites his opponent to join him in going wild, and a lurching, posturing mess of a fight often ensues. Hamed's balance is so changeable and he pulls away so awkwardly from incoming punches that even a glancing blow can cause him to flop about melodramatically, which makes an opponent overconfident about his own power. Tasting the unsettling force in Hamed's punches also encourages an opponent to look for a quick finish, and the irritating messiness of the fight angers him. A fighter who is simultaneously overconfident, scared, and angry is ready to be led astray. "Forget strategy," Hamed's style says. "Forget technique. Just try to kill me." Soon they are fighting his way. Now Hamed has the advantage, because he has neutralized his opponent's defensive technique and because he can land his own hard punches from any of the unfamiliar angles and awkward positions that a sloppy fight tends to produce. Kelley's ring experience might help him to resist Hamed's seduction — or, since Kelley's previous fights had taken shape around the traditional tacit compromise between combatants, it might not help much at all.

The two featherweight heroes put on a memorable show at the Garden in December 1997. Kelley started out well, but by the end of the night the television commentators were comparing Hamed's American debut with the Beatles'. Late in the first round Kelley retreated into a corner and covered up, setting a trap; the Prince leaped after him, throwing punches. Kelley, bending over out of harm's way, carefully switched his feet to get into right-handed position, then surged out of the crouch behind a looping right. Hamed felt the counterattack coming and strained backward, but it was too late and his hands were too low. The punch clipped him on the chin, depositing him on his backside in midring. The crowd threw a collective fit; Kelley raised his gloves triumphantly as he went to the neutral corner; Hamed got up. In the second round, Kelley earned credit for a second knockdown when Hamed yawed sideways so crazily after being hit that his gloves touched the canvas. Kelley was building up a commanding early lead in points, but it was hard to tell whether Hamed had been hurt. Hamed's odd balance amplified the apparent effect of Kelley's punches, but it also prevented them from landing flush with full leverage.

Kelley felt that he was about to knock Hamed out. Dispensing with craft, he sought a quick finish, a mistake for which he soon paid when Hamed caught him coming in and knocked him down with a short right hand. Kelley, reposing on the canvas on one elbow like a grandee at a picnic, pointed a glove at Hamed as if to say, "Okay, that's one for you. Now we'll see." It was still only the second round. Kelley remembered to box and move in the third, but in the fourth the two went at it like Godzilla and Rodan as the crowd filled the Garden with a solid block of continuous noise. They exchanged knockdowns; again, Hamed seemed only to lose his tenuous balance for a moment, while Kelley, who had excellent balance, went down hard because he was hurt. Hamed dropped Kelley a second time in the fourth with a left-handed counterpunch to the temple. Kelley waited until the referee had reached eight in his count, then tried to rise, but the temple shot had scrambled his balance. He did not make it. After six knockdowns and a great deal of drama, all compressed into less than twelve minutes of boxing, the Prince had arrived.

*   *   *

In March 1998, three months after the Hamed-Kelley fight, I took the Number 7 train out to Flushing Meadows, in Queens, to visit a comfortably broken-in Police Athletic League gym known as the One Ten, where Phil Borgia sometimes trained fighters.

When I got there, a dozen young men representing a variety of weight classes and ethnicities were preparing to train in fairly cramped quarters. As they wrapped hands and began to get loose, they discussed a recent episode in which Chuck Zito, a one-time amateur boxer and ex-con who had made the switch to Hollywood tough guy via bodyguarding the stars and onscreen stunt work, had reportedly knocked out Jean-Claude Van Damme at Scores, a strip club in Manhattan. Zito, in his early forties, had played bit parts in movies and had recently landed a more substantial role on *Oz*, the HBO prison show. Van Damme, who was a lot cuter than Zito, had achieved action-movie stardom with a combination of kickboxing expertise, a Franco-Arnoldian accent, and a "Muscles from Brussels" physique. According to a fighter at the One Ten, who sounded like he knew a guy who knew a guy, "Zito got up to go to the bathroom, and Van Damme was talking shit about him. When he got back to the table somebody told him about it. So he was like, 'What's up?'" The narrator enacted his idea of Zito's side of the confrontation, assuming the "are we about to have a problem?" pose: hands out, head cocked sidelong, chest and shoulders tilted forward, inviting an escalation. His listeners were particularly interested in the next part — how the disparity in styles and experience produced a quick KO. "See," the narrator explained, "he didn't give him *room*. Kickboxers got to get their legs, like, *unfurled*, you know? But Zito was right on him, two-punch combo: boom boom! It's not like in the movies." The narrator said, "Van Damme was all *lahk zis*" — the last two words delivered in an approximation of Van Damme's accent — as he flopped down on a mat and assumed the fetal position to demonstrate what a celebrity looks like when he's getting an ass-whipping. It was a good performance, managing to imply an entire scene: the spilling drinks and breaking glass, the stripper's studied dance form falling apart as she stops to watch, the shouting and then a little pause for the hitting, then more shouting.

Phil Borgia called his charges to order in a semicircle facing him. He led them in a series of preparatory exercises that mixed elements of traditional boxing, Asian martial arts, yoga, and Borgia's own inventions. They would deep-breathe together and slowly exhale while performing a stretch, then each came out of the stretch doing a freestyle burst of shadowboxing. In the short breaks between exercises, one of the participants, a brawny shaven-headed guy in black who wore a tiny gold silhouette of a handgun on a gold chain around his neck, demonstrated arcane street-fighting techniques to a couple of interested boxers. He grabbed a volunteer and put him down in an awful, spine-bent position, but without applying pressure, then let him up as the whole group, including the victim on the floor, animatedly discussed fine points of the throw-and-mangle move. When the shaven-headed guy switched to coaching a

tall young boxer in the mechanics of a flying whip-kick, Joe
Davis, an older trainer who works with Borgia, yelled,
"Hey! That's my heavyweight! Cut that out. You'll hurt a
leg or something."

After warming up, the group got into the ring, across
which Borgia had strung a rope on the diagonal from corner to corner at chest height. The fighters advanced in single file along the path of the rope, each bending his knees
and bobbing his head from one side of the rope to the other
while throwing punches. They were working on the art
of punching from the advantageous angles produced by
side-to-side movement. The erstwhile whip-kicking heavyweight had trouble coordinating the two motions, so Kevin
Kelley, wearing old sweats and nailing every detail of the
workout with a diligence that his younger and less illustrious colleagues did not fail to notice, took him aside and
went over it with him. At the end of the workout, the
young heavyweight made a point of thanking Kelley, with
heartfelt formality, for the lesson.

While Kelley stretched again and dried off, Borgia came
over to talk to me. He still had the Hamed fight on his
mind; it was his job to dwell on it. "The game plan,"
Borgia said, "was to break Hamed down," to box with rigorous correctness and let the flaws in Hamed's style create
openings. "We talked about it for ten weeks. If Kevin
dropped him ten times, it still wouldn't be enough. He just
had to jab, move, just box." But knocking down Hamed
the first time, even more than being knocked down by him
the first time, had encouraged Kelley to depart from the

plan and go for the knockout. Advancing without caution and forgetting to jab in his eagerness to throw bombs, Kelley had let Hamed get too close to him, neutralizing Kelley's superior technique and advantage in reach. "It's the warrior syndrome," said Borgia. "The Matthew Saad Muhammad syndrome." He was referring to the tendency of some dead-game fighters with sound boxing skills to abandon technique, shapeshifting lycanthropically into brawlers who win exciting fights and inspire the fans' love by accepting several doozies on the kisser in order to deliver one of their own. In the long run, those fighters lose more than they gain: their skills atrophy; they begin to lose bouts that they could have won by boxing rather than slugging; they suffer extended beatings, cheered on by crowds expecting their pulp-faced hero to pull out one more one-punch comeback; they survive in the business too long on guts and will; they get punchy.

Kelley had not yet slid too far down that blood-slick slope. "Kevin always learns from his mistakes," Borgia said, and he could still beat Hamed in a rematch by sticking to the plan and jabbing the Prince even sillier than he already was. "If I were Kevin Kelley," Borgia said, "I'd fight him in Yemen, in his backyard, in his mother's womb. Just to kick his ass." I asked how you get your fighter to stick to the plan. Borgia shook his head; he didn't know. Joe Davis, who was listening in, also shook his head; he didn't know, either.

When the trainers went off to close up shop, Kelley came over. He is a vigorous little guy (the featherweight limit is

126 pounds) with close-cut receding hair and an expressive, mobile face. He talks fast, and from time to time he thumped me on an available body part — forearm, shoulder, chest — to accentuate a point.

He was contrite about screwing up against Hamed. "Look," he said, "the bottom line is that I deviated. I pulled away from the plan. I know that. Fighters are emotional humans. I wanted the KO, I thought it was easy. I got knocked down, I wanted it back. Instead of jab and cross, I threw a lead. I wanted to kill him." He should have listened to his trainer, in other words. But he drew a different lesson from the result than Borgia did. "The first two rounds, I proved to myself he wasn't what he thought he was. I wanted to show *him* by KO'ing him. I thought he was ready to go. He was all like this" — he imitated Hamed, wide-eyed, backing up, looking as if he realized he was in over his head with a pro who could both outbox and outpunch him. In that moment, said Kelley, "I saw him shattered." The vision of the celebrity laid low, his aura dispersed by a sound craftsman, led Kelley astray. "I made a mistake," by which Kelley meant the tactical mistake of leading with his left, "and he took advantage." So, I said, next time you'd box him? Borgia, who was on the other side of the room, would have been horrified to hear that Kelley was not ready to say yes, exactly. Kelley said, "People always ask me, 'Why do you brawl when you can box?' I don't know, it's something inside of me. I'm not a warrior by choice, I'm a warrior by nature." He thought about that for a moment and seemed to decide he did not like the way it sounded — too instinctive, too fated. So he offered the opposite answer: "I brawl when necessary, when I have to. A fighter chooses styles like he chooses underwear or food. I was boxing Hamed, and I chose: it's time to brawl. I chose wrong. It's yin and yang." So, next time . . . ? "Next time, I'll brawl wisely."

When we got to talking about Hamed's celebrity, I began to see more clearly why Kelley had, as he put it, deviated. "Hamed is putting on a show," Kelley said. "Hamed, Jordan, Tyson, they're not athletes, they're celebrities. I want to be a celebrity. As a celebrity, I'd mean more to more people. There are stages in boxing, and Hamed is the last call. He's got a whole country behind him." He meant that the Prince had reached the apex of the fight game, where it obtrudes into the culture at large. The fantasy of not only beating Hamed but replacing him at that apex, of graduating from respected fighter to entertainer, had contributed to Kelley's desire to shatter him rather than merely to outbox him. When the Prince went down the first time, surprised by a switch, Kelley began to think about a spectacular early KO, the celebrity in the fetal position at his feet, the notoriety that would follow. He began thinking about being a star. "I can't afford to be entertaining, or to think that way," he conceded. "I just happen to be entertaining when I do my job. Nine-to-five people see me as a normal guy. They want me to kick somebody's ass."

But knocking Hamed out in the first round, while it would have made Kelley a major hero in the fight world, would not have made him a celebrity beyond its borders.

He was a remarkably tough little guy with exciting fights to his credit, and he had already won considerable fame in the fight world, overcoming the significant handicaps of being a nonheavyweight and a family man who lived quietly outside the ring and usually remembered to jab. But he lacked the self-importance and the willingness to let the media shape him that characterized Hamed or Ali. He wanted to be famous, yes, but he was too exacting a craftsman to abandon himself entirely to the felt demands of the television camera. When he talked about his plans to make the transition someday from fighter to television commentator, he said, "I'm a TV person," but then he proved he was not by adding, "I got chapters. If you see Hamed once, you've seen everything." Kelley believed himself to be the more effective on-camera entertainer because he had a lot more to say about boxing than did Hamed, whose public utterances were mostly repetitive sound-bite boasts. Unless Kelley overcame this naiveté, he stood little chance of making it as a personality on sports television.

I caught Hamed's act in person two years later, in August 2000, when he defended his sort-of-meaningful World Boxing Organization featherweight title in the Bingo Hall at Foxwoods against Augie Sanchez, a straight-ahead fighter out of Las Vegas. Hamed had fought and won five times since beating Kelley, but naysayers still said he was mostly flash and hype. He would receive his comeuppance, they said, if ever he stopped ducking the best men his size, especially the Mexican pocket-dreadnoughts Marco Antonio Barrera and Erik Morales. The flash and hype seemed to be working, though. His American fights were events: heavily advertised, attended by celebrities, well covered by the press.

Kevin Kelley was there, too. He had hired on for the evening as a commentator for BBC Radio. Wearing a sleeveless School of Hard Knocks T-shirt, he talked at ringside with Jim Lampley, the blow-dried blow-by-blow announcer for HBO. Lampley, who insisted that Kelley could achieve one last triumph in his upcoming fight with the fearsome Erik Morales, said, "He's a high-risk fighter, Kevin. He can be hit." Kelley, sounding considerably more realistic about his chances, said, "I just want to do something to close the door. Win, lose, or draw, I want to do something. I'm an artist. I don't *have* to fight." Later, I heard him comparing prizefighting to gunfighting. He seemed to be envisioning his bout with Morales as a grand finale, a chance to go down fighting, rather than an opportunity to pull off a stunningly redemptive late-career coup.

Everybody wanted to talk to Kelley that evening because he could offer a line on the Hamed-Sanchez bout. He had, of course, fought Hamed, and he had helped Sanchez train for the bout by playing the Prince in their sparring sessions. Kelley told the BBC that Sanchez was ready, mind and body together, but when asked for a prediction he shook his head, grimacing, and said, "I don't know."

An hour or two before the first undercard fight was scheduled to begin, Hamed came out of his dressing room to check the ring. Swaddled in blue sweats with a chevron insignia, he bounced on the ropes and tested the footing on the canvas in the sleepy, stylized manner of jocks who make theater of their preparations. He flashed a smile for the photographers at ringside, then performed a single shadowboxing move: he switched to a right-handed stance and threw a left uppercut followed by an overhand right. He held the pose after his follow-through for a moment, nodded, and left the ring. Soon after, the doors opened to admit early-arriving ticket holders.

I was sitting on a narrow platform about five feet above the floor, forty-five feet from the ring. It was designated for still photographers, but one could get up there with a writer's pass, and it provided a good vantage point from which to watch short guys fight. It was also the best spot available, because an influx of extra television people, VIPs, and international press causes ringside overcrowding at Hamed's fights.

The newspaper photographer next to me, a middle-aged, mustached, thick-built guy from Fall River, Massachusetts, wearing a USA ball cap, said he was pissed off that "some chick with a silicone job and a little point-and-shoot camera is up there" with her elbows on the canvas while he had to make do back here on the riser. She was some kind of VIP, so she took precedence over working press. He also groused about the pseudoevent quality of the evening's entertainment, produced by TV money and the promoters' inflation of a bad headline matchup. "Hamed's not that great," he said, "and this challenger's not that good. He's not even top-ranked." An hour later, my neighbor emerged from his funk when he spotted the guy who played Mini-Me in an Austin Powers movie. Exclaiming "Oh, shit," he rushed off to take his picture. Returning, half out of breath, he reported sighting a possibly famous rapper and hearing a rumor that Shaquille O'Neal (Maxi-Me, if you will) was there as well. The undercard fights were under way, but my neighbor was scanning the room for celebrities.

At 9:30, when the television broadcast started, the Bingo Hall was suddenly full; everybody was talking and carrying on, stargazing. Shaq never made it, as far as my neighbor could tell, but his NBA colleagues Ron Harper, Pat Ewing, and John Starks were there. So were Samuel Jackson, Denzel Washington, Wayne Newton, and at least three members of Aerosmith. Somebody called out, "The Sopranos are here!" as James Gandolfini and the others, all in character, swaggered down the aisle to ringside. A woman came up the aisle, shaking her camera overhead in one hand, saying, "I got Tony Soprano!" My neighbor, aroused, said, "How'd I miss them? How'd I miss them? I like those guys. I like that guy Furio. He's cool. I grew up with Italians. I love 'em." He went on to extol the virtues of Buddy Cianci, Providence's mayor, but he allowed that Cianci did show poor judgment in his criminal activities: "You don't shit where you eat." All this time, beginning well before the seats filled and the television cameras went on and the celebrities made their entrances, undercard fighters were beating the hell out of each other.

When it was time for the main event, Augie "Kid Vegas" Sanchez entered first, wearing a shiny silver and gold getup,

while the sound system played "Viva Las Vegas." Elvis im-
personators accompanied him into the ring, where they did
karate moves in homage to the King's fondness for martial arts. Then, after a restful Orientalist overture with the
house lights down, Hamed made his entrance. The music
acquired a dancehall beat and segued into a rap as spotlights played across a sort of entrance-to-the-mummy's-
tomb edifice at one end of the Bingo Hall. Hamed appeared
there amid flashpot effects, cascading dry-ice smoke, and
the tinny pop-popping of indoor fireworks. It looked cheap
in the way that the styrofoam boulders and bedsheet togas
of an Italian Hercules movie look cheap. Hamed did his
dance for what seemed to be a very long time before pimp-
ing to the ring, where he made a show of getting ready to
do his flip, then did the flip. Sanchez's faction had forted up
their man in his corner, turning a wall of backs to Hamed.

Hamed won the fight in his usual way. Sanchez, boxing
correctly from a conventional stance, stuck to his plan in
the first two rounds, taking few chances and scoring well.
He shook Hamed with straight rights to the body and
hard lefts upstairs, knocking him down cleanly in the second round — although the referee, perhaps befuddled by
Hamed's chaotic presence, ruled that Sanchez had stepped
on Hamed's foot and waved off the knockown. Hamed
gradually made the fight sloppier by seeking odder angles,
switching stances, and fouling. He found openings to land
punches, the force of which loosened Sanchez's grip on the
bout and dragged him further into the Prince's domain.
With about thirty seconds to go in the fourth round,

Hamed's flailing coalesced in sudden precision as he executed the move he had rehearsed in the ring hours before: switching to a right-handed stance, he threw a left and a right, which both landed flush, then a crushing overhand right for good measure that caught Sanchez defenseless in midair on the way down. Sanchez hit the canvas hard, half rose, then collapsed and stayed down for several minutes before being carried out on a stretcher and taken to the hospital.

I caught up with Kelley as he left the Bingo Hall. He said, "Augie didn't have the power. You have to get Hamed's attention. He wasn't moving Hamed with his punches. When I hit Hamed, he got all" — he wobbled around on spaghetti legs to illustrate the point. Kelley had felt Sanchez's lack of power when he sparred with him. "He's not a hard enough puncher. When I hit people, I shatter them." He would have elaborated further, but Cedric Kushner, the prodigiously fat fight promoter, loomed up in his path and hugged him. The featherweight nearly disappeared in the folds of Kushner's clothing and blubber.

At the postfight press conference, Hamed, who had nasty-looking marks under both eyes, covered his standard talking points. He gave all credit to Allah: "I had a smile on my face, knowing Allah was going to make me victorious to*night.*" He preached his own marketability: when you see a Hamed fight, he said, "you see explosion, you see a phenomenon, you see a guy getting knocked out. You're guaranteed drama and excitement, you're guaranteed music, and then guaranteed a knockout explosion." He talked up his opponent in order to confer more glory upon himself: Sanchez had come in well trained and with a good plan, Hamed said, and Sanchez had hurt him and knocked him down, but the Prince was a winner, a warrior, the best featherweight on earth. "I ain't no joke," he said. "I deserve every bout out there." If Barrera and Morales would only stop ducking him, he would take care of them, too. Hamed was amazed at his own greatness. "That was a devastatin' knockout," he said, and he had to laugh.

Whether Hamed was ducking the Mexicans or vice versa, the ducking finally came to an end. Hamed, still unbeaten, met Marco Antonio Barrera in Las Vegas in April 2001. As antiroyalists had expected all along, Barrera gave the Prince his comeuppance. Barrera has classical boxing technique, but he also has experience both in drawing skilled opponents away from their technique and in failing to draw them away, so he knew Hamed's routine and how to cope with it. He circled left to cancel Hamed's left-handed power, he jabbed steadily, he countered with left hooks when Hamed tried to hit him, he landed short rights to the body when Hamed gave him an opening. Most of all, he stayed calm and ignored everything about Hamed except his punches. Barrera stoically weathered Hamed's hard shots, but just as important, he did not give in to the urge to go for the kill when Hamed's head-flopping seemed to indicate that he was hurt. Barrera broke form just once, in the final round, when he frog-marched the Prince across the ring in an awkward clinch and bounced his head off the

padded ring post, pro-wrestling style. The referee deducted
a point for that, but Barrera was already well ahead on the
judges' cards. Hamed had been decisively beaten.

I called Kevin Kelley in Las Vegas to talk about the fight,
which he had covered for the BBC. "After the fight," he
said, "Barrera's people came over and said, 'Thanks for the
game plan.' Barrera watched my tapes, 'cause I exposed
Hamed. He relies on your attack, uses your force against
yourself. You throw, he counters, but then you got to
counter the counter." Kelley had revised his view of his
own bout with the Prince, now three and a half years behind him. "He won the fight, but he lost the war. When I
knocked him down in round one, I shattered everything
that was the aura of what he brought to America, everything that he said he was: the greatest, et cetera." I asked
Kelley to imagine himself as Hamed's trainer; what would
he teach the Prince? "Defense," he said. "His offense is
fine, except he has to learn a better jab, a forward jab. But
defense — he has to learn to tuck his chin and stop dropping his hands." He would teach Hamed to "finish combinations defensively," which means to come out of punching motion in balance and with one's hands up. "He's too
wide open," Kelley said, "and he doesn't move his head
when he punches." Kelley would make a better boxer of
the master showman, in other words, although he himself
was trying to do the opposite.

He had moved to Las Vegas, where he was concentrating
on his television career. "I might fight when I feel like it,"
he said, "but broadcasting is my number-one love now. Being on TV is what it is. I started in radio, but I love being on

television. I think people love me on television because they can see that. There's energy, it's exciting, whether it's boxing, acting, talking, whatever. It's all *being on TV.* I think my boxing status has helped my celebrity status, but I'm bigger now than I was when I boxed, because I'm on TV more." He was the ringside analyst for *KO Nation,* HBO's boxing series designed to attract younger viewers by surrounding the fights with a show: a live deejay playing up-to-date beats, a crew of female dancers doing up-to-date moves, and a buffoonish host, Ed Lover, who could speak directly to what the network hoped was a vast constituency of young, action-craving, baggy-pantsed dudes piled six-deep on their couches in front of their televisions. As "the only boxing person on the show," Kelley said, his job was "to solidify it, to give it that boxing weight" without acting as a drag on its uptempo pace. He had worked hard to routinize his natural hyperactivity as an onscreen persona. "My energy level," he said, "it's like I'm gonna blow, like *I'm* gonna fight." Building his second career would take more such work, he recognized, but he was eager to succeed. "I'm a lot better broadcaster than I was back in the day," he said. "I'm as ambitious to be a broadcaster as I was to be a fighter." I asked why. "A broadcaster has a lot of power," he answered. "Like Larry Merchant" — the dyspeptic analyst for HBO's regular boxing telecasts — "he's been trying to retire me, spreading rumors about my eyes. Merchant judges everybody; I give my opinion."

So, now that Kelley's first career was ending, I asked, how did he want to be remembered as a fighter? "I want people to remember me as a different breed," he answered, as a hybrid ideally suited to entertain in the ring: "boxer-slugger, lefty-righty, boxer-fighter. I'm a wolf in sheep's clothing. The two styles that I liked when I was learning to fight were Jeff Chandler, who was a great boxer, and Matthew Saad Muhammad, who was totally the opposite. I wasn't just a boxer who could slug, I was a boxer-slugger. That's what I want to be remembered as." In his view, nobody remembered a fine technical boxer who defended himself and won decisions. People remembered wars, and the warriors who fought them. "The fights that I won easy, hands down, even against great fighters, the public don't care about those fights. They talk about me and [Troy] Dorsey, Gainer, Hamed. The public wants to know how you take it. The avid boxing fan doesn't want to see a fighter that never gets hit." As he saw it, he had brawled wisely, winning fame without abandoning craft. "That's the line I'm drawing, between competitiveness and getting hit too much," between exciting fights and gory incompetence. "I didn't get in to slug. Never. I got in to win. But the bottom line is what the audience wants." He saw himself, in retrospect, as an entertainer with boxing chops. "And I was more than a fighter," he added, "I was a politician," by which he meant that in the 1990s his charisma had done much to build an audience for boxing on cable television, especially HBO's *Boxing After Dark* series.

Television did not appear to be returning the favor. *KO Nation* had been a bust; it would be canceled soon after we talked. Kelley had some other possibilities to pursue on television and radio, and he was planning to lend his name to an Internet sports-quiz game, but he had not yet managed to execute the switch from boxer to entertainer. He was still hung up in the zone of transition, where a switcher can get hurt.

A few days later I called Phil Borgia. He had moved to Las Vegas, too. "I wanted to look out for Kevin and end his career with him," Borgia said, and he was running the Academy of Fighting Arts for Rock Newman. I asked him about Kelley's embrace of brawling in the latter stages of his career, and about Kelley's justifying the transformation on the grounds that it provided a better show. Borgia teaches fighters how to outsmart and outwork opponents, to hit without being hit, so what did he think when Kelley put aside his teaching and waded in throwing telegenic bombs? "Look," he said, "sometimes he doesn't listen. Kevin is my son, my brother, my best friend. He's grown as a man and as a fighter in this business. He's got his own mind. Yeah, it bothered me that when he was 41-0, people were in his ear, saying, 'You're a robot, you're more exciting than this,' and maybe he listened to them. But it's not bad that he's gonna take his own way, and I can't be mad at him. You have to respect age, experience, a two-time world champion."

After a pause, he said, "I've known Kevin a long time." Twenty years earlier, the fourteen-year-old Kevin Kelley had asked his father to take him to a boxing gym. They tried one on Long Island, but it was too far from their home in Flushing. Then the two of them happened on the One Ten one evening, right there in the neighborhood. "I had the lights on," said Borgia, "the music blasting, we were in there training, having fun. And they just said, 'Let's try *this.*'" In the two decades of collaboration that followed, Borgia had thrown everything he knew into Kelley's education, including the power switch, the turnover, which Borgia claimed to have invented. "It's *my* thing," Borgia said. "You let the opponent commit weight and energy, then we take that spot away with the switch. All we need is that split second to cut the distance on the change with that choppy step. The key is knowing how to make it end in the power zone. Boom. Good night, Irene. It's high risk, but there are high rewards."

The switch had become an increasingly important part of Kelley's style in his late career, but it was not a tactic he could depend on, especially as his speed faded. In the first round of his rematch with Derrick Gainer in July 1998, for instance, Kelley had tried a switch and Gainer, timing it, had dropped him to one knee with a counter. Gainer went on to beat him handily. In September 2000, Kelley had done what he could against Erik Morales, but the younger man had won nearly every round before the referee stopped the fight in the seventh. ("They stopped it too early," Kelley told me over the phone, "but he was gonna get it. I was gonna switch on him.") Interviewed in the ring just after the fight ended, Kelley said he had been bothered by leg cramps, which prevented him from doing his switches. He also took the opportunity to tout an upcoming *KO Nation* broadcast, sliding into a pitchman's voice with an air of wry self-consciousness as he turned away from Larry Merchant to speak directly into the camera.

7

The Distance

When the ship bearing my grandmother, her husband, and their two sons arrived in America on the day after Christmas, 1951, Sandy Saddler was featherweight champion of the world and the celebrated lightweight Beau Jack was already past his prime.

Saddler, a slugger, took too many hard blows and gave them back in bushels. He and Willie Pep, a cutie pie, had already exchanged the title twice before Saddler beat Pep in September 1950 to regain it, then beat him again in September 1951 to retain it. Beau Jack (a.k.a. Sidney Walker, a.k.a. the Georgia Shoeshine Boy) was thirty years old in 1951. No longer one of the best in his weight class, he was still a man to be reckoned with. His free-swinging style had won him a loyal following at Madison Square Garden, and in the early 1940s he had won, lost, regained, and then lost the New York State version of the lightweight title; he had been in the army and lost some fights since then. He was always formidable in the ring — curiously deep-chested and broad through the body for a little man, fast and fearless in pursuit of his reedier opponents — but he could be had by a shrewd technician who did not make mistakes.

I have seen films of Saddler and Beau Jack in their primes. When I watch these fights — especially the ones they lost — I see how strong, how capable, both men were. I see all the resilience that was in them, the force of body and character that sent them back to the gym to train for the next fight. A half century later, when I saw Saddler and Beau Jack in the flesh as old men, these virtues were still at work in them, tempered by the beatings, hard lessons, and losses the years had visited on them.

I first went to the Fight Night charity event in Washington in October 1997. (I went back two years later to hang around with Earnie Shavers.) I was in town then for the American Studies Association conference, an annual event in which a couple of thousand academics and fellow travelers get together for four days of professional angling, mild after-hours conventioneering, and scholarly talks on subjects like "Toward a General Theory of How Things Mean" and "Harriet Tubman vs. Spider-Man: Who Would Win?" The proceedings provide both edification and joy in measured doses, but the climate in the hotel — both the physical airlessness and the undercurrent of anxiety generated by a thousand little career dramas of the who-is-talking-to-whom variety — does wear on a person. So, noting that a card of fights would be held at the Washington Hilton on one evening of the conference, I secured credentials and escaped down the hill, so to speak, to ringside.

I found the scene much as I would find it again two years later: the raised ring in the center of a sea of well-appointed tables; the tuxedoed donors, liking themselves best on this night of all nights, blowing clouds of expensive cigar smoke across fresh-cut flowers and calling for more drinks; the hostesses going purposefully among the men; the floor show; the mismatches in the ring.

After the undercard events, mostly simple affairs in which a fighter with a winning record beat the tar out of one with a losing record, Butterbean pummeled a shapely heavy bag named Ken Woods, whom he had already knocked out earlier in the year in Texas. Woods's thickly muscled body impressed the spectators, but he had no chance. He didn't know how to translate strength into leverage, and he had trouble managing his wind and balance. Butterbean knocked him down in the fourth and last round with a punch that hit him in the forearm, one of a series of majestically telegraphed hooks under which a half-dozen competent heavyweights could have ducked safely in unison. Derrell "Too Sweet" Coley, the winner of the other headline bout, was a skillful, evasive welterweight. He put on a fine display of footwork, defense, and judicious punching, winning almost every round from Romallis Ellis, a persistent scrapper out of Atlanta who couldn't catch

him. Coley, a local fighter, showed himself adept enough
to mix with a better class of welterweights, but he didn't
move the crowd because he didn't knock Ellis down or cut
him up.

Fight Night's usual variety of attractions and distractions had been arranged to supplement the fights. Jerry Lee
Lewis played a couple of tunes on an electric piano in the
ring. Sam Moore sang the national anthem soulfully, blowing only one line, "And the rockets' red glare," which he
rendered as "And the daybreak in air." (Something about
boxing matches seems to addle singers of the national
anthem. Once, at the fights in Allentown, a guy named
Mookie with a gorgeous Lou Rawlsian voice lost his way
right after "O say can you see." He paused, said "Oh,
God," paused again, and then free-associated through the
rest of it.) Michael Buffer, the tower of unction who has
turned himself into a celebrity by repeating the phrase
"Let's get ready to rumble" (pronounced "ha-LLLET'S GET
READY TO RUMMM-BULLL!"), handled the emcee duties
with his trademark blend of bark and purr.

The evening's other attraction, occupying a middle
ground between boxing and show business, was the group
of distinguished former champions collectively referred to
as "the legends." The recently retired heavyweight Riddick
Bowe was nattily suited and bearded, gigantically impas-
sive; he wore little round glasses that seemed to say, "Don't
ask me about a comeback. Can't you see I don't get into
fights anymore?" Despite having grown over the years
from a welterweight into a light heavyweight, Sugar Ray

Leonard had kept himself trim, with an active fighter's sureness and ease of movement. Ken Norton, imposing in a dark suit and a black Panama hat, still bore the marks of the steady hammering he took in his crablike advances on Muhammad Ali and Larry Holmes. There was the once svelte but never spartan Ingemar Johansson, who relieved Floyd Patterson of the heavyweight title with an Asgardian straight right in 1959 and then suffered stern beatings in return bouts against him. Now Johansson peered out of several prosperous decades' worth of extra battening like a man in a space suit. The lumpy faces and banty carriage of Carmen Basilio, Gene Fullmer, and Jake La Motta told the story of their tenures in the late 1940s and 1950s as middleweight champion and their encounters with Sugar Ray Robinson, who beat and was beaten by all of them. Sandy Saddler and Beau Jack, now in their seventies, were the frailest. Small and stooped, they walked with difficulty.

Except for the photogenic Leonard, the legends were not exactly celebrities, since most people in attendance had only the vaguest conception of who they were. Rather, they were tradition incarnate, principal figures in the evening's historical pageant. The aura of a bygone heroic age surrounding them was reinforced by the cigarette girls with their outthrust wooden trays and wheedling patter, the wives left home with the kids, the rolling clouds of cigar smoke, the hoisting of strong drink in the company of one's guildsmen, and the barnstorming Butterbean — whose crude skills, planetary girth, and good-natured showmanship evoked a dimly remembered order of potent fat men who traveled with carnies and fought all comers in the century before television changed the world. A hint of horse-and-wagon antiquity always drifts in the air at an exhibition of the manly art of self-defense. "Look at the *noses* on them," a well-oiled fellow with well-oiled hair muttered loudly to an associate as Fullmer and Basilio passed nearby. "Those fucking guys are old school." The time and damage tallied in the faces and postures of the retired fighters helped transport the crowd to a semi-mythical era that most of its members would be too young to remember.

After Lewis sang his numbers, before Moore sang the anthem, the legends were introduced one by one. The house lights came down and the crowd grew quiet. Each man climbed into the ring in turn and stood waiting, a straight or a bent silhouette in the dimness, while Buffer listed impressive achievements and closed with a ringing flourish — something along the lines of "and tha-REEE-time CHAMpion of the WORRRLD . . ." When the name was finally announced, crisscrossing spotlights caught the man at the center of the ring, and he waved to the applauding crowd before heading to a neutral corner to make room in the center of the ring for the next hero.

I had been watching Sandy Saddler and Beau Jack with some concern since the round of cocktail parties that preceded the evening's events. They both moved slowly, Beau Jack leaning on a thick cane and Saddler taking tiny steps, head down, always with a helper at his elbow. They sat together during the parties while the others mixed and joked, and the pair showed signs of liveliness only when Sugar

Ray Leonard came over to say hello. They reared back at his approach and smiled, making little noises of recognition and delight. Their suits hung off their necks and wrists, making the two men seem interchangeably frail. When they got up into the ring, though, I saw the difference between them.

Beau Jack mounted the steps to the ring apron all by himself. Even with somebody obligingly holding the ropes apart, it's difficult for an old man to bend and step cleanly into the ring, but Beau Jack levered himself between the ropes without faltering. When the spotlights hit him, he grinned toothlessly, his mouth working, and raised his hands to the crowd in a gesture that was both gracious and triumphant. When he did that he let the curved handle of his cane slide down his forearm and catch in the crook of his bent elbow. It was the only time I saw him standing without assistance. When he was done mitting the crowd he went carefully but with all possible speed to the ropes, like a fighter who has been hit and hurt. Once there he grabbed the top strand for a long moment to steady himself, then turned to put his back to the ropes, readjusted his cane, and stood among his peers. I realized that he had been saving himself all evening for the trial of this introduction, managing his energy so that he could acquit himself of his public responsibility. He had seen the evening whole from the outset, like a distance fight, and he had measured his expenditure of self accordingly.

Saddler had much less energy in reserve, and he spent it all getting into the ring. He climbed the steps to the apron with assistance from fellow legends and functionaries, and somehow he got through the ropes. Once in the ring he stood — bent into a question mark, head deeply bowed, but standing alone — during Buffer's description of his exploits. But when the time came to cross the ring under the spotlights he could not move on his own. Eventually Ken Norton, who had already been introduced, went to him, took him by the arm, and helped him across the ring to his place with the others along the ropes. It took an excruciatingly long time for Norton and Saddler to cover the distance, long enough for the lights to go down and then up again as Riddick Bowe entered the ring, was introduced, and went to the ropes. The sight of Norton, not known for his gentleness, bending solicitously and taking miniature steps to match Saddler's made the older man seem all the more diminished. Like Beau Jack before him, Saddler clutched the ropes when he reached them, but he could not stand unassisted. Someone passed a chair into the ring for him to sit on during the rest of the introductions and the national anthem. When it was time to leave the ring, Beau Jack and the other legends filed out through the ropes and down the steps, but Saddler balked. The last man in the ring, he stood there facing the ropes, head down.

Saddler took hold of the top strand and hung on as legends and functionaries took turns leaning close and whispering anxious encouragement to him. It was a delicate moment. Norton had climbed back into the ring and posted himself at Saddler's elbow, and now he exchanged a look with Bowe, who was standing on the floor along the ring apron, reaching up between the strands to support

Saddler's unsteady legs with his huge hands. It would have been easier just to pick him up and pass him over the ropes, but only beaten, injured fighters leave the ring that way, carried by others. As a champion, as a member of the fighters' fraternity, as a man whose dignity was at stake, Saddler had to go out *through* the ropes, on his feet. Still, the gala evening was threatening to grind to a stop.

Saddler's insistent grip on the top strand became the focus of attention at ringside. A well-dressed younger woman, his daughter, joined the knot of men at ringside to plead with him. Having gotten nowhere, they began to pry his fingers one at a time off the rope. They did this carefully, politely, apologizing with their faces as they broke what was left of his strength. Until then I hadn't known it was possible to pry someone's fingers politely. When they had loosened the one hand, however, they realized that Saddler, with the resourceful desperation of a wobbly fighter scheming to survive the round, had secured a grip with the other hand. They had to start over on the other hand while gently preventing him from getting the first one back on the top strand. Once they had both hands free they eased him through the ropes, protecting his head, like cops ushering a suspect into a cruiser. Saddler left the ring on his feet, supported and swiftly propelled by a dozen helping hands, and in that dreamlike floating state he passed almost without effort down the steps and to his table. Nobody could blame him for doing what a fighter has to do when he has spent himself in the ring. He had gone to the ropes, clung to uprightness, lasted out the distance.

*   *   *

The expansive donors in their tuxedos had manliness on their minds. They saw their own virtue as providers in the money they had raised that night to pay for unspecified nurturant women to care for many poor, defenseless children. They saw the elements of some atavistic ideal of manhood in the fights and the pageantry surrounding them — in everything from the trophy women on display to the resonances of a violent domestic history in Jerry Lee Lewis's nickname, "The Killer," which they shouted appreciatively. They responded to the legends as exemplars of male dignity, old-school champions who had given and taken their beatings like men. Taking in the scene from the intimate detachment of press row at ringside, like a naturalist privileged to witness a complex ritual involving swell-chested hooting among male penguins, I could not help but think of my grandmother. The evening's pervasive nostalgic impulse took this curious turn in me early on, at the cocktail parties, when I saw the older gentlemen engaged in a struggle I thought of as hers: to get through an important ritual occasion in one piece.

I caught a startling glimpse of her in the champing motion of Beau Jack's mouth as he stood, excited and straining, at ring center. I could see her in the way Saddler's bony shoulders squared and then drooped under the dark fabric of his suit when he stalled in front of the ropes, out of gas but determined not to be rushed into a mistake. I could see the calculations of her old age in the way the young fighters paced themselves in their bouts, saving and expending themselves. Boxing is not just fighting; it is also training and living right and preparing to go the distance in the broadest sense of the phrase, a relentless managing of self that anyone who gets truly old must learn. Seeing Beau Jack and Sandy Saddler on Fight Night helped me understand my grandmother, oddly enough, and, perhaps odder still, she helped me see where the old men found the strength to get up into the ring one more time.

Begin, as always, with the ring walk: the protagonist enters, surrounded by resonant artifacts and her seconds. When my grandmother died in 1995, she had every postcard and letter she had ever gotten from back home in Sicily and Eritrea; she had receipts for utility bills she paid in the 1950s; she had archived her family's passports, report cards, photographs, and union cards, and the chest x-rays and affidavits that attested to their good health and character when they immigrated to the United States; she had stockpiled Bibles, missalettes, laminated cards bearing prayers to various saints in Italian and English, parish newsletters, and letters of thanks from the orphanage in Sicily to which she had sent small donations over the years. Distributed around her small house in Flushing were a dozen worn purses, each loaded for Mass with a small Bible, a prayer card or two, and a tiny change pouch with no more than seventy-five cents in it; when it was time for church she could grab the nearest purse and go. It took a crew composed of her two sons, a nephew, and a grandson three days to clean out her house when we sold it. As I went through her belongings, separating them into piles destined for charity or the family or the trash, I set aside the Catholic buckshot for myself: all the tiny plastic and silver crosses, the statuettes of the Virgin Mary, rosaries made of wood or glow-in-the-dark plastic, medals and stickpins and earth and holy water acquired at sacred sites from Lourdes to Chicago. These cheap, homely items hold the charge of a long, hardworking Christian life.

After the ring walk comes the introduction. Perhaps I should do it the way Michael Buffer would: "This seamstress, born Maria Maio in 1905 in Barcellona, Sicily, married Sebastiano Rotella, a carpenter, in 1928. They moved to Asmara, in Eritrea, in 1938, and to New York City in 1951. They had two sons, Vittorio and Salvatore. After her husband's death in 1966 she lived alone in their small and increasingly cluttered house in Flushing, Queens, until her own death, at the age of eighty-nine, in 1995. Ladies and GEN-tlemen, the author's late GRAND-mother, a CHURCH-going CHA-RISSS-tian woman, FIVE-time grandmother, and ONE-TIME GA-GREAT-GA-RAAANDMOTHERRR: MARIA ROTELLA!" Picture her standing at ring center, bent but black-haired to her dying day, appreciative of the *rispetto* but finding the spotlights too harsh. She would have worn her ratty old fur coat for the occasion and made a sketchy wave to the crowd before saying "Okay, *basta*" and heading for the ropes.

In her Sicilian hometown, my grandmother came to be known in the 1970s, 1980s, and 1990s as a paragon of traditional virtues. She had not lived there since departing for Africa in 1938, but she had siblings, cousins, and in-laws in profusion in Barcellona. The town is thick with Rotellas and Maios. When my grandfather died she took his body back to Sicily to bury him. After his death she returned to Barcellona every fall and spent a month visiting his grave. She visited with the living in the evenings, but the point of the trip was her daily walk up the hill that led from the businesslike, unpicturesque town to the sun-kissed cemetery, a place of quiet Mediterranean loveliness. The cemetery is also thick with Rotellas and Maios, blocky men and hard-handed women looking forthrightly at the camera in oval black-and-white photographs that adorn the graves. In the stone necropolis, a more compact and serene version of the town, the dead are dignified and patient; down the hill, the living are always angling at each other and taking offense.

My grandmother owned the plot next to her husband's, in a good location on the cemetery's central pedestrian avenue, and she kept the property spruce and orderly during her visits. People in town — Sicilians making their way into an Americanized age of divorce, heroin, and Nintendo — could direct one another's attention to the old woman, turned out in dark clothes of once stylish cut, climbing the hill to the cemetery. They could say: See? She's going to put flowers on her husband's grave. She lives in America, but she's still old school. Why aren't you like that? (She came back for good in 1995: a loose column marched up the hill in the sun, past saluting policemen; a band playing drunken-sounding dirges led the way.)

After her husband's death, my grandmother's annual trip to Sicily became the central event of her year. Once she got good and old, aging neck-and-neck with the century, the journey increasingly took on the galvanic, all-absorbing character of a title fight. This was after her joints and arteries and eyes started troubling her, after she had to stop sewing professionally, after she suffered a couple of bad knockdowns: she broke her hip when she fell out of a tree she was pruning, and she was leveled by a thief who ran off down the block with one of her Mass-ready purses dangling from his arm and his platform shoes clacking, like a woman late for a bus. In her last years, she got into the habit of answering my greeting of *"Nonna, come va?"* (Grandma, how's it going?) with a doleful self-parody: *"Sono vecchia e piena di dolori"* (I am old and full of pain). She had to be at graveside in Barcellona on November 2, All Souls' Day, and it took the better part of two months to ready herself for the effort it would require to travel there. She needed to store up energy to endure the airports, the train stations, the meals prepared by strangers, the visits with old friends and relations — all the extra steps and necessary courtesies that ate up her reserves.

So every September she started to cut back on her movement through the already austere geography of her world. She put off housework and let the big flowering bushes in front and the tomato, hot pepper, and basil plants in back fend for themselves. She stocked up on prescriptions and food, so she would have her pills for the trip and so she could stop making frequent trips to Key Food — she called it *Kifu,* infusing the supermarket's dingy aisles and wobbly-wheeled shopping carts with the air of a Mediterranean island. Most important, she cut down on her attendance at church. St. Nicholas Tolentine was a few blocks from her house, requiring a walk up 164th Street to Union Turnpike and then over to Parsons Boulevard. These were the only streets whose names mattered to her; she called them *Ahunnasixateefortastreet, Toinapika,* and *Aboulavard,* waving her hand in a shooing motion to indicate distance and effort when she invoked them. Going to church was like making the trip to Sicily in miniature — it was the central event of her week — but in September and October she went to church only on major saints' days; otherwise, she said her prayers at her various makeshift shrines at home. Anybody with eyes to see, God included, would know she had to save herself for the coming effort. In December, when she was back from Sicily and staying with my parents for the holidays in Chicago (where, she said, the fruit lacked savor) or California (where the fruit was okay but the sun was "too white"), we would drive her to church and she could go every day if she wanted to.

For most of the year, the weekly struggle to keep up the house and the garden, shop at *Kifu,* and go to church was an important part of what kept her alive. She stayed in shape for the business of living, using herself up so that she would remember how to make more of herself. But she also needed to rest, save, and ration herself, to recognize and work within her narrowing limits. The energy she stockpiled in September and October would get her to Barcellona and the cemetery. Once there, if she had correctly paced her training and traveling, she would have enough left to get up and down the hill every day. Those walks, combined with eggplant-intensive Sicilian cuisine, the grudgingly respectful ministrations of her extended family, and the not inconsiderable sense of doing the right thing, would nourish rather than destroy her. When she returned to America in December she would recuperate from her travels while visiting us for the holidays, looking out the window and growing progressively more bored without a full day's work to do. Come January she would be ready for the daily routine in Queens.

She used to drive me crazy with her balancing act. The older she got, the more she avoided wasting energy standing in line or taking unnecessary risks occasioned by politeness. She went straight to the cashier at *Kifu* or the drugstore, ignoring a dozen customers waiting their turn. I smiled awkwardly at them and they made a universal shrugging, eye-rolling signal — What are you gonna do? — of impatience and understanding. When pedestrians passed near her on the sidewalk, or when cars rolled up to the red light and stopped as she crossed *Toinapika,* she would stick her hand out in a panicky gesture, as if to fend off the threat. At church she followed a certain path to a certain pew, and if other parishioners were in the way she put her head down and shuffled at them. Especially when she wore the fur coat, which made her resemble a woodchuck no longer spry enough to steal vegetables from gardens, she was the archetypal little old Sicilian lady, perhaps the last one in the neighborhood. The stylish young immigrants from Asia and the Caribbean who had come to dominate the congregation stepped aside to let her pass with the extra solicitousness accorded an endangered species, a ghost, a legend.

My grandmother had most of her life arranged on a horizontal axis, eliminating confrontations with staircases and escalators, but when she did encounter an escalator she usually stalled in front of it for a long minute or two. This happened at the airport twice a year, every year. A wedge of shrugging, eye-rolling, watch-checking travelers with their bags would collect behind her while she stood there, head down in concentration, gripping my shoulder and tentatively jabbing one foot at the treacherously uneven moving surface. She was like a fighter with failing reflexes who sees an opening but can't summon the will to move decisively into it. Even with my back turned to the crowd I could tell they wanted me to pick her up and put her on the escalator. Eventually I settled on a procedure that entailed first putting her suitcase on the escalator (it would be sitting there when we got to the other end, but her departing belongings acted as a sort of mechanical rabbit to get her moving), then grasping her firmly under the near elbow and around the far shoulder, timing her next jab-step, and taking most of her negligible weight when she rocked forward so that she sailed onto the moving stair and balanced, with my help, on one foot until she could get the other foot under her, too. We did something like that again at the other end. It would not do to suggest taking the elevator. Once we had confronted the escalator, it was a matter of pride to deal with it. She had to conserve effort, but she also had to protect herself — that is, her dignity — at all times. Even a minor indignity like being defeated by an escalator held within it the awful possibility of becoming someone else, the kind of person to whom such things must happen. Humiliation was as bad a waste of herself as chasing after a departing bus or making an unnecessary trip to the drugstore in mid-October.

I lived in or near New York for the last thirteen years of my grandmother's life, and I used to visit her once in a while. Mostly, she talked and I ate. Before I left, she would give me a jar of sauce and a plastic tub of cooked pasta, the whole thing securely wrapped and tied up in several plastic bags. She would walk me to the front gate of her yard and stop there, a hunched figure in the gloom, while I went up *Ahunnasixateefortastreet* to the bus stop on the next block. It's a very wide avenue, lightly traveled and desolate at night. Her little grandmotherly house was on a corner; across the side street was some kind of satellite receiving station, its giant dishlike structures tilted up to the heavens behind graffiti-splashed fences topped with razor wire. The juxtaposition made my grandmother in her front yard look impossibly tiny and alone in an increasingly forbidding world. When I got on the bus I would take a seat on the right side so that she would see me when I passed by her house. She was holding tight to the top of the metal gate with one hand, wrapped up in something dark to protect herself from a chill, waiting to wave as I went by. The first few times I did this I felt silly waving back to her, since everybody on the bus was looking at me with my parcel of leftovers, but eventually I got used to it. I even got in the habit of saying "*Ciao, Nonna*" to the window when I waved, then turning to my fellow passengers as if to say, "That's my grandmother, folks. So sue me." Like the crew at the One Ten gym, a busload of people in Queens often includes a dozen nationalities and ethnic groups. All of them agree that respecting your grandmother is a high form of human endeavor. Sometimes I would catch strangers — say, a Filipina nurse and a West Indian woman with shopping bags — exchanging a look across the aisle: See? A nice boy visiting his grandmother. Look at all that food. Now *that's* an old-school grandmother.

I knew my grandmother was dying when she started letting me help clear the table. Before, she wouldn't hear of it. It was important to her to do the extra work of buying meat at *Kifu* to feed me, preparing the meal and cleaning it up herself, and seeing me to the front gate. These were ways in which she showed what mattered: family, in this case, and her continuing capacity to do for herself and for others. As when she walked to the cemetery in the fall to tend to her husband's grave, she was doing something eminently practical, but she was also pouring a vital part of herself into the forms and usages of ritual. In doing these things she both used herself up and made more of herself — a woman with a family, a story, a place in the world — to expend next time. She did the same thing when she toiled the long blocks to church, expending herself for her God but also reinforcing her sense of herself as a Christian woman, with the duties and privileges appertaining to that status. She had a habit of stopping in front of one of the stations of the cross. She would touch two fingers to her lips and reach high to touch them to Jesus, repeating the sequence three times. Walking to church to perform that rite was a struggle, but struggling for what mattered helped make her the kind of person who would have the wherewithal to get to church next time and perform it again.

The flashes of my grandmother's gestures and habits that I saw in Beau Jack and Sandy Saddler helped me to see what those two old men were doing at Fight Night, and why they might have traveled so far to enter the ring one more time, with nobody to fight and nothing, apparently, at stake. It was not just for the recognition, although surely the crowd's applause and Michael Buffer's swooning tones reinforced their sense of who they were. It was not just for charity, although surely the cause of raising money for the good of children mattered to them — just as it mattered to the cigar-smoking emperor penguins, who (in their more detached and tax-deductible way) also poured something genuinely of themselves into Fight Night. Entering the ring is the central event of a boxer's life, the act that separates pugilist from gym dabbler, the moment when a boxer is poised between a lifetime of preparation and a world of hurt. The prefight ring walk, like my grandmother's walk to *Kifu* or to church or to the cemetery, offers a compressed rendition of the fighter's path through the larger world. It's a practical necessity — how else should an able-bodied person get from the locker room to the ring? — but it also suggests what might be at stake in the fight. That is why, during their ring walks, fighters surround themselves with flags, belts, costumes, slogans, music, friends, family — all the accumulated furnishings of a life story. Climbing through the ropes one more time, Beau Jack and Sandy Saddler were doing the same thing they had done in their immortal youth, when they trained tirelessly and fought great opponents now long dead. A half century later, the two old men were still choosing their battles, still balancing regeneration against exhaustion. Like my grandmother making her way steadily up the hill with the energy she had saved for the occasion, they were showing themselves prepared to go the distance.

8

Bidness

LARRY HOLMES stood at the ropes in the ring, harangu-
ing a pair of lawyers who had stopped by his gym to watch
him train. The two visitors, both short and soft, had the
look of Lehigh Valley big shots: winter tans from Florida
or a salon, sport jackets that fit poorly at the neck and
butt ledge, stretch slacks and loafers. When they came in
they had hesitated self-consciously just inside the door-
way, looking over the room and marshaling the appropriate bluff heartiness. A slight awkwardness in one's public
manner, even if one is a big shot, marks the local style — a
touch of the loathing for fancy self-regard on which the
nearby Amish have built their way of life.

Holmes, wearing a sweat-soaked gray T-shirt and skintight electric-blue leggings, was finished sparring. His cor-

nermen had divested him of gloves, foul protector, and headgear. As Holmes approached fifty, his sparring sessions had become more measured, even contemplative, but this afternoon's had turned mean. Shouting encouragement to his initially recalcitrant sparring partner, Linwood Jones, Holmes had walloped him thoroughly. Holmes had made effortful punching sounds — *Huh-huhgh! . . . Yoop! . . . Layoop!* — as he threw combinations, a sign that he was hitting in earnest. Jones, hard-pressed, had fought back with more than feigned aggression, and the action had been unusually fast and fierce. At the end of the last scheduled round, Holmes had said, "Now you got to go one more because you hit me in the back of my head," and in the extra round he had landed hurtful body punches with his breakable right hand, another sign that he meant business. The next fight in his long-running comeback was still more than a month away, but his fighting disposition, like his technique, needed tuning up before a bout.

Holmes had been warming down in the ring by himself when the lawyers came in; he interrupted his shadowboxing to give them a hard time, too. He held one or both, and perhaps the class they represented, responsible for not selling a piece of his property as quickly and lucratively as he would have liked. "It's not making any *money,* goddammit," he told them. "What the hell these lawyers *for* except to make me some money?" The visitors sat in folding chairs at ringside, looking up through the ropes at his imposing figure. They wore smiles meant to show that their colorful pal did not fully comprehend the complexity of such matters.

Holmes pointed down over the ropes at them with one wrapped and taped hand. He said, "That market's gonna fall soon, a big fall." The smiles grew wider and thinner. "What's gonna be left that's worth something? Property. That's right. Real estate, real property. So take care of my goddamn bidness like you're supposed to." Holmes says "business" when he wants to, but when he says "bidness" he means not just his financial affairs but also the whole unsentimental history attached to his name — a story of laboring in the gym, in the ring, and at the office for many long years to earn the right not to take any shit from anybody. Having said what was on his mind, Holmes let the moment pass. He offered a hard peacemaking laugh, echoed uncertainly by the lawyers, and went into a circling and jabbing routine. As he shadowboxed, he added, between breaths, "My mama always said, 'Use your head. It's the little things that count.'"

The lawyers, deciding they had not been insulted, sat back in their folding chairs, relieved. Each hauled a loafered, black-socked foot over a stretch-slacked knee, the pant leg hiking up to expose the pale calf above the sock line; their jackets gaped and settled. Holmes moved in the ring, sticking and countering an imaginary opponent.

On another afternoon at the same winding-down hour, still unretired and a few months closer to fifty, Holmes was messing around in the ring at the end of a workout when somebody asked him about the continuing Frazier-Ali feud. Holmes said, "Why should Joe Frazier be mad at Muhammad Ali? Every time he fought him, he made five million dollars. That's fifteen million dollars. If you give me

fifteen million dollars, I'll kiss your ass in Centre Square."
An observer sitting for a few days among the idlers on the
benches around the Civil War monument in Centre Square,
the traffic circle in the middle of downtown Easton, could
count on seeing most of the town's inhabitants pass by. In
the imagination of a resolutely local man of the Lehigh Valley like Holmes, there is no stage more public than that,
not even the television screens and national publications
where Frazier and Ali have conducted their extended beef.
Holmes said, "I'll let you fuck me in the ass in Centre
Square for fifteen million dollars. They can call me a fag-
got, and I'll say" — here he affected a high, effeminate
voice — "thank you very much." Still in that high, effeminate voice, he called out "Bye now," turned and waved
over his shoulder like Audrey Hepburn departing in a road-
ster, and climbed out of the ring.

"People talk about 'I love boxing.' That's bullshit,"
Holmes said, making a face, as we sat in the offices of
Larry Holmes Enterprises in the L & D Holmes Plaza on
Larry Holmes Drive, three quarters of a mile from the gym
and a couple of blocks from Centre Square. It was July
2000; he was fifty years old. "Boxing is bidness, that's what
it is. Bidness." This is his official ideology, and it comes in
two complementary pieces. First, "Boxing taught me a lot
about business. Any time you deal with boxing, you got to
learn business. You make some money in boxing and you
don't know anything about business, you ain't gonna have
no damn money. Because when them guys get through with

you — all your friends telling you different things, the promoters handle your money before you handle it, you're getting it at the end — if you don't know nothing about business you ain't gonna have it. Business teach you how to say
no. A smart businessman always says no. That way, he
keeps it a little longer." Second, and conversely, business
has taught him about boxing. "In boxing, my style is business style. Hit and don't get hit. Stay out of the way of the
dangers, and that's business-wise. The object is to hit and
don't be hit. But most of the guys out there, they just go out
there and whale away. And that's what happens to their
money. They blow it, they live a fast life."

Holmes had not blown it. Following his mother's advice,
"Buy land, 'cause they ain't gonna make no more," he had
invested his earnings primarily in real property. As of that
moment, after he had sold off a hotel and some undevel-
oped acreage, his holdings in the immediate area included a
big house at the edge of town with a boxing glove–shaped
pool, the gym where he trained, older rental properties in
downtown Easton, and 78,000 square feet of office space
in the two recently built brick-and-glass buildings of the
L & D Holmes Plaza (the D stood for Diane, his wife).
His office was on the second floor of the building that
also housed his restaurant and his wife's lingerie shop; the
other building's tenants included a U.S. district court, about
which he liked to say, "I'm the only black man in America
who owns his own jail cells." He distrusted the stock market (he preferred municipal bonds), but he did allow himself to gamble in casinos and to pursue iffy minor ventures,

like an Internet gambling site advertised with his name. He also owned some nice cars and a couple of fishing boats. It was an opulent life for a guy who stood in line for government cheese when he was growing up, but for a rich man in America it was nothing fancy. "Thanks to Easton," he once said, "my lifestyle has been at a minimum."

Belt and Suspenders: The Larry Holmes Story is not a movie coming soon to theaters everywhere. Having done Muhammad Ali to its own satisfaction, Hollywood will heedlessly trample Holmes underfoot in its rush to get to Mike Tyson's raging psychodrama. Posterity tends to reduce Larry Holmes to the champion who, in one writer's words, "made boxing seem strictly an act of commerce." Bracketed in the sequence of heavyweight all-timers by two media dreamboats — a champion who made boxing seem like political theater and one who makes boxing seem like nonconsensual sex — Holmes has been overshadowed.

He may be intermittently bitter about being eclipsed by the two leading celebrity boxers of the television age, but he has helped bring that relative obscurity upon himself. What material does he offer for the assembly of conventional stories about a prizefighter? He is neither cute nor monstrous, neither overweening nor pathetic, neither earnest nor brutish, neither invincible nor doomed, and he does not claim to represent any cause other than the well-being of his immediate family. He still has his money and he still has what he calls "my functions": his speech might blur slightly now and then, but he is more thoughtful and articulate than he was when he took up boxing in the late

1960s. He has said that he would gladly trade his place in history for cash on the barrel right now. What would the tag line of a Larry Holmes biopic be? "He took the money, went home, and lived prudently ever after"?

His pragmatic boxing style makes no concession to popular tastes, either. Ali made a fetish of speed and prettiness when he was on the rise, and then, during his long decline, of his capacity to take like a man the beatings he had escaped in his youth. Tyson fetishized volcanic punching power and anger: during his rise the combination made him dire; on the way down it made him a self-destructive hothead. But Holmes, on his way up and on his way down and in between, just kept hitting the other guy, blocking and slipping return punches or interdicting them with well-timed jabs, rolling with the blows that got through his guard and weathering those that landed flush. Patient and hardy, he kept his attention squarely on the task at hand (which can be hard to do in a boxing match, as both Ali and Tyson discovered to their sorrow), and he stayed true to the bedrock stylistic principle of defense with bad intentions. "I got to box a guy," he said, meaning that he made up for his lack of one-punch knockout power by meting out incremental punishment round after round. "My thing is I always make 'em drunk, then I mug 'em."

That's how Holmes defeated ironclads of the 1970s like Roy Williams, Earnie Shavers, and Ken Norton. He put Ali out to pasture, too. While keeping one eye on Don King, he held the title for a remarkable stretch of twenty fights from 1978 to 1985 (a reign second only to that of Joe Louis), during which he outboxed a whole generation of promising heavyweights, including Mike Weaver, Scott Le Doux, Trevor Berbick, Leon Spinks, Renaldo Snipes, Gerry Cooney, Tex Cobb, Tim Witherspoon, Marvis Frazier, Bonecrusher Smith, David Bey, and Carl "The Truth" Williams. By the time he retired in 1986, he was entering his late thirties and past his prime. His record stood at 48-2 after two inconclusive and piscine encounters with Michael Spinks in which Holmes first lost the title by dubious decision and then failed to regain it by even more dubious split decision. He unretired in 1988 to fight Tyson, who knocked him out, then he went on retiring and unretiring throughout the 1990s. During this extended comeback, fighting into and through his forties as his weigh-in figures rose from under 220 pounds to almost 250, he lost title bouts by decision to Evander Holyfield and Oliver McCall (and ringside judges did him wrong in Denmark after he easily bested Brian Nielsen), but he had beaten everyone else — nineteen men by the summer of 2000, some of them decades younger than he — to bring his record to 67-6.

Perhaps the choicest Holmesian moment of these comeback years, a late-career masterwork, was his defeat of Ray Mercer in 1992. At the time, the unbeaten Mercer was a leading heavyweight with the best chin in the division. He hurt people, and nobody could hurt him. Beating Holmes would give Mercer another credential as he angled for a shot at a major title and the big money. But Holmes, at forty-two, with most of his reflexes and stamina long gone, fought the perfect old man's fight and spoiled one more rising star's trajectory. He made close to a million dollars, too. Since he didn't have the legs or the wind to work briskly for a whole round, Holmes would land some jabs to get ahead in the judges' estimation, then set himself up in a corner. When Mercer attacked him there, Holmes would hit him with rights and smother Mercer's punches in his long, entangling arms. Holmes expertly husbanded his limited resources for twelve rounds, making small but decisive shifts in spacing and leverage to keep Mercer out of step and out of position to do damage. At times, the younger man stood there stymied, his head jerking as he took punches, trying to think of something else to do. Mercer should have taken away what was left of Holmes's energy by hitting him in the body, but he kept trying to knock his block off and never succeeded. After losing by lopsided decision, Mercer said, "The better man won tonight," and added that he had learned his lesson. Asked what that lesson might be, he responded, "I gotta learn how to box."

By the summer of 2000, Holmes's triumph over Mercer and his last chances at a piece of the heavyweight title were already years behind him, but he still wanted to fight. He was running out of worthwhile opponents, though. Titleholders, contenders, and those with even an outside chance of becoming contenders would no longer have anything to do with him, since he could only make them look bad. Holmes had the wherewithal to find an opponent's flaws, and getting beaten by him would ruin a career. A good fighter could probably defeat Holmes just by staying busy in every round, but there would be no glory in beating a fifty-year-old, even a distinguished former champion. So leading heavyweights refused to fight him, and he couldn't make much money fighting obscure ones, since those matchups wouldn't rate a television contract.

That left him with two options. One was to fight old men like himself whose names evoked the heavyweight golden age of the 1970s. He had recently beaten Bonecrusher Smith (again, fourteen years after he did it the first time) and acquired a bit of fluff called the "Legends of Boxing" title, and he was trying to arrange a Twenty Years After rematch with Mike Weaver. But the only possibility of a multimillion-dollar payday was to fight George Foreman, who had returned to the ring in middle age and knocked out champion Michael Moorer. As an advertising pitchman and ringside commentator, Foreman was always on television, and a Holmes-Foreman matchup promised to have TV appeal of the same kind as a *Good Times* reunion special. It even had some interest as a boxing match, offering the starkest possible stylistic confrontation between the two best examples of master boxer and booming puncher to be found on the shortlist of all-time heavyweight greats, with the action conducted at a stately pace that would allow casual sports fans to follow its tactical nuances. Holmes had been trying for years to get Foreman into the ring with him for a last hurrah, and they had been close to a deal a couple of times in the 1990s, but now it was too late. Foreman had grown too rich and had fallen too far out of fighting shape. A couple of million dollars was not enough incentive for him to endure being jabbed in the head two hundred times by an opponent on whom he would probably fail to lay a glove.

The other option was Butterbean, perhaps the only marketable pugilist who could gain credibility as a boxer by fighting Holmes. As he approached the age of thirty-five, Butterbean had lost some of his good humor and allowed his celebrity to go to his head. No longer content to reign as the King of the Four Rounders, a novelty act, he parted ways with his Bay City handlers and set out to become a legitimate heavyweight. That meant he had to fight somebody who could fight back, and he thought Holmes — august and venerable — would serve as a suitable gatekeeper. The two camps were discussing the prospect of a fight somewhere down south. From Holmes's point of view, there was no reason not to do it. The stubby-armed Butterbean was as slow as Foreman, his punches were heavy but not sharp, he had no footwork or defense, and he had no experience against competent opposition. Holmes figured he would jab a little, move a little, avoid some easily avoided punches, ram his elbows into Butterbean's mushy biceps when the two men tangled up close, and go home several hundred thousand dollars to the good. Even if the fight went the distance and the judges robbed him of the decision, even if Butterbean landed a lucky punch or two, it seemed like an easy payday. (It turned out to be just that. When they finally met in July 2002, Holmes soundly thumped Butterbean and received almost no punishment in return on the way to a ten-round decision.)

*   *   *

Still, a Holmes-Butterbean fight felt wrong in a pearls-before-swine sort of way. Nobody goes around proclaiming that Larry Holmes is the best heavyweight of all time, but in his prime he was as good as anyone who ever lived — not better, necessarily, but as good. Reviewing the all-time roster of heavyweights, from the bare-knucklers of the nineteenth century to the canonical champions of the twentieth to the body-beautiful giants of the twenty-first, I can't think of anybody, ever, on whom I would confidently bet to beat Holmes in a dream matchup of fighters in their prime.

"I never got a chance to be in my prime" in a fight, Holmes told me. He insists on this in the same way that he insists boxing is business. He allowed that he was close to his physical prime when he fought Earnie Shavers the second time, in 1979, the time Holmes got up from the canvas like a guy building a house in a storm who gets blown off the roof, wraps duct tape around his broken ribs, and climbs back up to finish the job. He said he might also have been close to prime when he got ready to fight Ken Norton for the title in 1978, but then he pulled a muscle late in training, which prevented him from using his right arm much. The Holmes-Norton bout was a rugged classic, featuring a memorably brutal and suspenseful fifteenth round in which the two men dropped all pretense of fistic art and laid into each other like bighorn sheep. But Holmes gave me to understand that if he had not been fighting one-handed he would not have let Norton last that long. He believed that he had never been exactly right on any single fight night, that there was always a catch, an injury, an opponent who did not bring out the best in him. He said, "I show my talent more so in the gym workout than I did in the actual competition." In his preferred self-portrait, he was at his best when working on his craft in the shop-floor gloom of the gym, not when putting on a show under the lights on fight night.

If that's so, I proposed, let's imagine that when you were at your best in the gym — let's say during the first half of your reign as champion, when you were at the peak of strength, speed, and health, but also ring-wise and in full command of your powers — God had put before you the best heavyweights of all time, in their prime, for you to fight in fifteen-round bouts in front of impartial, open-minded judges. Let's start with Louis, since many people say he was the best of all time.

"There could only be one Joe Louis," he said, and he gave thanks that he had not been born in Louis's time, when it would have been even harder for him to make his way in America than it had been in his own time. Pious disclaimers out of the way, he got down to cases. "I'm not gonna knock against Joe Louis, but in my opinion I kick his ass." Louis was the best in his time, Holmes acknowledged, but he was an offensive-minded fighter who could be hit. "In my time, when I was fighting as champion of the world, they could not touch me. They couldn't lay a hand on me." He half laughed at the thought of all the murderous punches he had foiled. "I had the skills, I could take a punch when I got hit — and that was something that never happened to me, hardly, that I ever got hit." As for Louis,

"He follow you around," meaning that Louis would walk right into Holmes's jabs. "I had the kids in the gym last night, they were doing the same thing": sitting forward in his desk chair, he squared his shoulders, put a dull expression on his face, and mimed plodding one-twos. Holmes, shiftier and more mobile than Louis, and armed with the longer, harder, and more unpredictable jab, was confident he could take the guy apart at long range. "Bang, bang, bang, hit him all day long with the jab." I objected that Louis was not that stiff, that he had a fine jab of his own, but Holmes cut me off, saying, "He would paw at you, throwing it, to get you around, then — whop! — hit you with the right hand. But you ain't gonna *be* there."

How about Rocky Marciano? "I wouldn't even need a plan," Holmes said, "because, what I've seen of him as a fighter, he's what you call a face fighter. He fights down — 'scuse me for my demonstration." He rose from his wheeled desk chair, pushing it back, and shambled across the wide stretch of wall-to-wall carpeting in a knuckle-dragging parody of Marciano, hunching forward, grunting, throwing crude blows with alternate hands. Holmes suddenly straightened up, turned to face the troglodyte he had just impersonated, and speed-evolved into himself: circling one way and then the other, pausing to throw left jabs and the occasional right cross or uppercut, employing his advantage in reach to maintain a distance between the fighters at which only Holmes could score. As he punched, he asked, "What do you think a Larry Holmes like this — whop, whop, whop — would do to a guy down here *like this?*" He dropped his voice to a Neanderthal basso on the last two words as he switched back to being Marciano for a moment, then he returned to his classical stick-and-move style and his own voice, into which entered a passionate throb as he said, "No way in hell can he beat me. Just move — whop, whop — move — whop! Hit him all day with the jab."

Holmes, a grandfather with a spreading midsection, was wearing chinos, a black polo shirt bearing the logo of a nightclub he used to own, and steel-gray glasses, but when he began to stick and move he looked just as he always has in the ring. Big through the body and arms, but deceptively light on his skinny legs, he fired the jab before or behind the beat on which one might predict its arrival, dropping bombs with the right in a similarly unpredictable pattern.

When he was done beating Marciano, and as long as he was up, he did a dead-on impersonation of Jack Johnson's archaic milling-hands technique. "Now, he's more my style. Guys like that cause problems." He put the young Ali in the same category; prime Sonny Liston, too. "Liston probably could be the best, the biggest problem, because he could jab, and he was straight up, and he knew how to cut the ring off, and he kept his hands up real nice." These are Holmes's peers: fast, creative heavyweights with skill to match their talent; big enough to hurt a man with any punch, take his best shots in return, and shove him around in the clinches. The rest of the all-timers — pile-driving lummoxes like Foreman, technicians like Gene Tunney and Jersey Joe Walcott, surging advancers like Jack Dempsey,

Frazier, and Tyson — would all be so much meat for the prime Holmes's grinder. He could fight them only in his dreams, of course.

One can go around and around, head over heart and vice versa, in considering these fantasy matchups, and in the end who knows? It's a speculative parlor game, a matter of punching at phantoms. There can be no pretense of systematic objectivity in any all-time ranking of fighters. For what they are worth, subjective rankings of heavyweights by various authorities these days almost always put Holmes in the top seven of all time, often in the top five and sometimes as high as third, below only Louis and Ali. I asked how he felt about his ranking's tendency to rise of late. While he sparred with ghosts we had ventured far from Butterbean into a discussion of style, not money, and now he seemed to bring himself to heel. Retaking his seat, he said, "As time has gone by, they starting to take a look at me, but it doesn't really matter that way. I mean, if they were *paying* me when they say I'm the greatest" — well, that would be different — "but they don't come with a check, you know?" Remember: boxing is bidness.

A minute later, though, he interrupted another train of thought to add, testily, "Only time I think about it is on a Sunday when they come up with me number two outside of Mario Andretti and them guys racing cars, when they're doing who's the greatest in the valley." He was referring to a local newspaper's end-of-the-millennium series on the Lehigh Valley's greatest athletes. Holmes did not like placing second to a white guy who worked sitting down, but more than that, he could not completely cover up how much he cared about his place in history. He means what he says about money, but he also uses money talk to screen another, less quantifiable part of his reason for fighting and winning: a deep investment in craft. "I love what I do," he said at last, with a kind of resignation. He loved his craft for its own sake, but he also wanted people to recognize how good he had been at it, how good he still was. "I care about my fame. I like it, okay? I like my status." There, he had said it: money alone couldn't explain why he fought.

He was admitting that he had been hurt when the local paper ranked him second to Andretti, and when Holmes is hurt he gets his guard up and concentrates on the fundamentals of self-defense. He said, "You know what I like better than all of that? I got it. I got money, I have my family, and I have something to show for all the work that I done. That's all that matters to me." Then, with mounting energy, he went back on the offensive. "People with celebrity status, they think that they gonna be able to look down from hell, or look down from heaven, and say, 'Boy, they talking good about me, it sounds as great as ever.' No shit gonna be like that!" I asked what it was going to be like. "How the hell do I know? But I'm saying dust to dust; the Bible says ashes to ashes, dust to dust." Back in his rhythm, the hurt behind him, he delivered the lesson's essence. "Listen, if I die today, there are gonna be a lot of crying people for about a week, then they gon' go on with their life. If I die today, and they having a fight in Madison Square Garden tonight, they ring the bell ten times and they keep right

202 ■ CUT TIME

on goddamn fighting. If I die today, you gon' walk out of
this goddamn building and have lunch somewhere, talking
'bout you just interviewed Larry Holmes. That's all it gon'
be, a more valuable interview. It's what you sell is what
you get."

Forget posterity; concentrate on the business at hand. He
felt that as he grew older he had become more disciplined,
not only about how he fought but also about why and
when to fight, and about what it meant to him. "I mean, if
you pull out in front of me in your car and I slam my brakes
on, I might say, 'You motherfucker,' but I ain't gonna get
out and punch you out." He got mad less often than he
used to, and controlled himself better when he did. If, for
instance, a writer twisted his words in an interview, "I'm
not gonna let you piss me off if you fuck me up in your
paper, 'cause that's what you want to write. I'll be like,
'Damn, you fucked me up, man,' but you know what? I
ain't gonna shoot myself in the head. I'm a little loud expressing myself, like I am now, but I know how to do. I
swear to God, I practice it." He said he would buy a guy a
drink to avoid a fight in a bar, or call the cops. He had no
interest in kicking anybody's ass to prop up his own pride
or build up his own legend.

But he would do it in the ring for money and, while earn-
ing that paycheck, for another chance to show he was still
good. Together, they were reason enough not only to fight
but to fight well. Neither business sense nor pride of craft,
by itself, could have turned a gangling young knucklehead
from Easton into the undisputed heavyweight champion of

the world. An unchecked craving for money eventually collapses into hunger for a free lunch, which makes boxers lazy and fat; a fascination with technique for its own sake eventually collapses into aesthetics, which, in a line of work suffused with ugliness, isn't always reason enough to persevere. But business sense and craft, intertwined, reinforce each other and add up to professionalism. Holmes may be the ring's best exemplar of that quiet virtue.

Before I left, we stood at his bank of windows and considered his view. The L & D Holmes Plaza overlooks one of the Lehigh Valley's most important vistas, the river junction where the Lehigh meets the Delaware. The valley grew from this hub, developing as a center of heavy industry along the rail lines and canals that converge outside his windows. The landscape, shaped by the demands of commerce, is beautiful in a functional sort of way: rusty bridges cross the broad, moving waters of the rivers and the still, narrow waters of the canals. Across the Lehigh we could see Easton's South Side, where he grew up and where his gym is. The Larry Holmes Training Center, a utilitarian building on Canal Street hard by the railroad tracks and the river, used to be a welding shop before he bought it in the 1980s with money he made fighting Tyson.

Holmes would be going to the gym later in the day to train. He would never get a chance to settle things with Louis and Marciano and the rest of them, of course, but he could still fight and there was still money to be made in the ring. He was good enough, he estimated, to beat 90 percent of the heavyweights out there at that moment. An opponent short on skill, stamina, or attention span would be in for a difficult time. So Holmes had work to do, on his craft and on his wind, which meant putting in a shift at the gym in the afternoons and running in the mornings — not as much as in the past, but enough to steel himself for long rounds against a younger man. Holmes, who would celebrate his fifty-first birthday the following November and knock Mike Weaver out two weeks after that, had been running along the towpaths of the Lehigh Valley's canals for more than three decades. "You can run forever," he said, "and never reach the end of them. Makes you strong."

9

Hurt

WHEN I FIRST started going to the fights, I always half
expected somebody to call them off. Even now, when I
have spent enough time at ringside to make boxing familiar
and sustaining, I surprise myself once in a while with the
realization that nobody is going to intervene. Usually that
moment of rediscovery occurs when a fighter suffers a bad
cut, or during an obvious mismatch in which the better
fighter hurts the other but can't finish him. I find myself
watching for someone — the referee, people in suits rush-
ing up the aisle with legal documents in hand — to stop the
fight prematurely, because we in the crowd can easily figure
out in our heads the calculus that the fighters are doing the
long way, showing their work. They are conditioned not to
give up, but sometimes I think I can read in the set of a

fighter's head and shoulders the wish for a third party's intervention to spare him further suffering, even if that means losing the bout and the chance to know whatever secrets the balance of it might have held.

Maybe I should save my compassion. An apparent mismatch can even out, as Andre Baker showed me one evening in Randolph, Massachusetts. A nasty-looking cut may not prove decisive, as Art Baylis showed me one evening in Allentown, Pennsylvania. A man in trouble can work out of it, as Larry Holmes did against Earnie Shavers or as Gary did when life floored him with a cheap shot in the form of James Haverinen's airborne car. Sometimes compassion can get in the way of understanding the developing inner logic of a fight. Almost everybody at ringside was worrying about Kevin Kelley's closed eye — the pain, the risk of permanent injury, the delicate matter of rescuing an over-the-hill former champion from himself without humiliating him — while he worked deeper and deeper into Derrick Gainer's range and timing, feeling for the moment to win the fight with a one-eyed switch leading to a one-punch knockout. More than one fighter has come back to win after his blood, sprinkled on my notes and shirt, has made me wish the referee would step in and save him. When that happens I feel a would-be meddler's guilt: had the bout been stopped when I wanted it stopped, he would have to cope not only with hurt but also with the defeat I wished on him. After winning, in the ring with his gloves off and his hands still taped, well-wishers and functionaries all around him, he looks especially satisfied to have persevered in difficult circumstances. He strikes a fistic pose for a ringside photographer — hands cocked, chin down, faint smile — and one can see that in this moment, anyway, he has the hurt banked inside him, like a bottled genie. For next time.

Boxers hurt each other on purpose, a simple truth with unsimple consequences. In boxing, hurt means more than nerves sending unpleasant signals (that's pain, what a baseball player feels when he fouls the ball off his foot) or damaged bodies becoming impaired (that's injury, what happens to a football player when he cuts left and his knee doesn't). In boxing, hurt is what people do to each other, an intimate social act, a pessimistically stripped-to-the-bone rendition of life as it is lived outside the ring. Hurting each other is all there can be between two boxers in an honest bout. Everything else about the fights, even the arresting moments of kindness, proceeds from that basic fact. It may look like parental love when a cutman and trainer labor tenderly over their fighter in his corner, for instance, but they do it so he can get out there and hurt the other guy some more. The primacy of hurt supercharges even the smallest detail — a feint, a totemic nickname, a thick gob of Vaseline on a fighter's cheekbone as he comes out of his corner at the bell — and produces the distinctive ozone crackle of bad intentions that attracts some people to boxing and repels many others. Anything that boxing teaches, anything it can say or be, must pass through the filter of its most basic fact.

Hurt changes you. There are potential lessons in getting

hurt by others, in hurting others, in seeing others get hurt. In that sense, hurt carries meaning; it can educate you, as I have been trying to show in one way or another throughout this book. But it can also rob you of your capacity to learn or feel, or even to think. A fighter who gets hit too often can descend into dementia pugilistica; a heavy hitter can go blood simple; a jaded spectator can fall entirely out of the habit of compassion, losing any feel for human consequences beyond the technical and the sensational. In that sense, the meaning can drain out of hurt, leaving only the nakedness of it. The tension between lessons to learn and the brutally wasteful finitude of lessons animates every fight — not just a title bout between well-paid celebrities, but also a mismatch between a future champion and a journeyman, a tank-town six-rounder between a local hero and a professional opponent, a twilight encounter between a former champion and a near-miss contender who will rise into only the second or third tier before receding into obscurity.

So, in lieu of review session, final exam, and valedictorian's address, I leave you with three more fights. Years after I saw them, I still find myself thinking frequently of them, not because they were extraordinary but because each says something fundamental to me about hurt, and therefore about boxing. Strung together, they form a sort of time-lapse composite: of a night at the fights, from undercard scraps to the main event and its aftermath; of a boxer's life, from youthful promise to an old age shaped by long-ago punches; of an education at the fights, from raw hitting

to the processes of learning to the limits of learning, beyond which lie mystery and just plain damage.

Spadafora vs. Andreske
Lightweights. 6 rounds.
November 21, 1996. Erie, Penn.

A rising young lightweight from Pittsburgh named Paul
Spadafora was wearing down his man. Spadafora had a
body like a blade, lean and tempered. His close-cropped
dark hair and his tattoos — a blue image of boxing gloves
on a chain dancing around his neck, and the word SOUTH
curving across his narrow stomach over the image of a paw
— suggested spartan self-denial edged with stylish self-regard. He was undefeated and he was very good — a future
champion, in fact — but he was still trying to master his
gift.

   After a round and a half of coping with Spadafora's
measured pursuit and rib-cracking body punches, Mark
Andreske, his red-faced opponent from Bay City, Michigan, knew he was out of his league. (Remember Bobby
Rishea, the prolific loser from Ontario who gets beat up in
Massachusetts all the time? Andreske had fought a four-
round draw with him a year before.) Ruefully settling into
the marathon of lasting out the fight, Andreske tried to
counterpunch and move, but Spadafora cut off the ring and
bore in on him. Forced to give ground, Andreske found
himself cornered with his back to the ropes. Spadafora

hunched his left shoulder in a feint and then shifted his weight smoothly to put it behind a right hook to the gut just above the armored point of Andreske's left hipbone. It made a complex sound — a stiff crack layered into a bass thump, with the crispness of something breaking and the resonance of depths plumbed. Andreske kept his guard up and his chin tucked over his left collarbone, but the rest of him seemed to flow around Spadafora's gloved hand even as he shrank, hurt, from the blow. Spadafora was finding and making regions of softness within his opponent's hard-trained abdomen, each of them aglow with deep, lasting pain. Spadafora considered for a moment, weaving gently in front of Andreske, then produced a well-practiced copy of the previous attack: he feinted a left and put another leg-driving, weight-shifting, gracefully arcing right in the same spot. As the two of them worked through the logic of the match — the one finding ways to deliver doses of force, the other trying to conserve his body's eroding integrity — I was thinking of Andreske's internal organs rolling and bruising in the lightless sea of his insides, like submarines bracketed by depth charges in old movies.

The most common image of damage in boxing is of blows to the head, which scramble the balance and wits both immediately and over the long haul. When a fighter stands up under a barrage of blows to the head, the damage does seem to be visibly accruing. But there are also many cases, especially in mismatches, in which a punch or two to the head ends it quickly, and what looks like a catastrophic event — the fighter collapsing as if poleaxed, with his legs going one way, his arms another, and his wits a third — is in fact a kind of salvation, because the fight is over.

Body punching is different. Once in a while one sees a fighter floored and finished by a body shot early in a fight, but usually such damage accumulates more gradually. Only after an opponent's energy drains away and his guard comes down will a dedicated body puncher's attention be drawn up to the undefended head; then the denouement is soon reached. In a fight between equals, though, or when the superior fighter is a good body puncher but not an adept finisher, body punching develops over the course of what seems like a very long time indeed.

Watching a body puncher at work, one feels with special force the sense of life-changing, soul-altering hurt. The cruelty of it proceeds in part from the fact that the damaged party, if he is diligent and courageous, shares the responsibility for his own suffering. Because boxers devote such effort in training to hardening their middles against punishment, it takes a sustained attack to break them down. Having in his brief, undistinguished career done hundreds of thousands of situps and run thousands of miles, having learned to stay on his feet when hurt and to get up when knocked down, Andreske had ensured that the first eight or ten body punches would not finish him. He had guaranteed himself several rounds of punishment before reaching the moment of collapse. If he caught a few breaks and landed a solid blow or two in return, he might last out the fight.

Andreske did not make it. He lasted through the third and fourth, punching less often and grabbing for Spadafora when he could. Spadafora showed flashes of awkwardness when he moved his punches up to the head, so there was no quick finish. (Spadafora was a committed body puncher back then. But in later years, as he developed into a contender and then a champion, facing better opponents who were not so easily hurt by his sharp but not particularly heavy punches, he increasingly concentrated on winning rounds on the judges' cards with defensive wizardry and rapid-fire combinations to the head.) Finally, in the fifth, he knocked Andreske down with a body shot. After Andreske took his count and got up, Spadafora knocked him down again. The second time Andreske fell, he spun wildly into the ropes, his body loose and open. He rose again, game, but the referee stopped the fight. It was, by the book, the right time to stop it. Right after the first knockdown would have been too soon, since when Andreske got up he had been able to sustain his guard and throw punches. Even so, some part of me had wanted the fight stopped just after that moment in the second round when Spadafora's two rights to the body had told all of us everything there was to know about the beating to come.

Graffius vs. Vega
Junior middleweights. 6 rounds.
April 11, 1997. Allentown, Penn.

The locally prominent lawyer who promoted fight cards at the Days Inn in Allentown also announced the action for the regional cable television service. On fight night he wore a tuxedo; the TV lights imparted a rich shine to his black pompadour and beard. Unlike most of his peers in the regional stratum of the fight-promoting business, he had a reputation for regularly matching hometown fighters tough, although fans enjoyed themselves just as much when he gave them a mismatch. Despite the presence in nearby Easton of Larry Holmes, the Lehigh Valley crowd of racecar devotees, hunters, and high-school-wrestling buffs showed little interest in the finer points of boxing and seemed content to watch specimens of local manhood perform what amounted to bayonet practice on semi-animate mannequins imported for the purpose. When the lawyer brought in a live one, though, it created the possibility for a local fighter — and perhaps an attentive spectator — to learn something.

I had never heard of Jeff Graffius, but the fact that he was fighting out of Pittsburgh gave me some hope that he would give a good account of himself. The Pittsburgh fighters I have seen on the Pennsylvania mill-town circuit are often competent and hardy, a good combination. The lawyer and his matchmaker, hunting for an opponent for the local hero Mike Vega, might have seen only futility in Graffius's record of 8-30-1. But they also might have noticed that Graffius had fought the state's most talented fighters at his weight, a much better class of opponents than Vega had encountered. There was always a chance that Graffius had discovered something about his craft in all that fighting.

When the fighters got up in the ring I was further encouraged. Graffius was a friendly-looking, unexcited guy of about thirty with a blond crewcut. He had a broad neck that flowed down into rolling shoulders, a deep chest, thick arms and thighs, and tapered calves; everything was joined in a balance of motion and power, without the fuss of cabled veins and pebbled musculature that comes with fanatical weightlifting. He did not seem to have any seconds at all. The bald, mild-looking gentleman arranging the bucket behind him had worked the corner of another fighter, from Maryland, earlier in the evening, and appeared to be working Graffius's corner as a courtesy. Graffius punched the air a couple of times, swung his head to loosen his neck, and pronounced himself ready to go. He looked like a guy who would walk a hundred miles or hitch a ride with malevolent drifters, if he had to, to get where he needs to go. He had lost thirty fights, but nobody was going to hurt him.

Vega, meanwhile, was bounding around the ring, flicking jabs, kneeling in a neutral corner for five seconds to pray, winking at a friend in the crowd; he was already into the faking and twitching he would employ during the fight. He had a tight rangy body, drawn tighter by prefight nerves. Even his hair was taut; it looked like wire. Vega was a head taller than Graffius, but so lean by comparison that it was hard to believe they were in the same weight class. He was only 4-6-1, despite being well over thirty, but he had proven he could hurt a guy. A few months before, I had seen him knock out a weak opponent in the first round.

The man, dropped by Vega's first solid punch, went to sleep instantaneously in midair, his chin on his chest and his feet dangling as if from a hammock, then crashed to the ring's floor in the worst way: first his spine struck, then the back of his head.

Once the fight started, Vega jabbed furiously, changing directions as he circled the ring, doing everything in double time; Graffius, patiently advancing, was like a man driving posts in bee-filled woods. He came on, gloves high to absorb Vega's punches, trying to get within range to deliver a double jab with his left. When Vega's moving and jabbing disrupted this advance, Graffius would shake his head, stop, and start again, unhurried. They went around like this for most of the round, then Graffius managed to land a hard jab that sent Vega backward a half-step toward the ropes. Graffius paused for the smallest of beats to establish the correct spacing between them — one could almost feel the click as he fell into the maneuver's familiar rhythm — and then threw his first overhand right, a steer-killing blow to the temple. Vega went to his knees with a look of contrition on his face and then pitched forward, as if fainting in church. He got up unsteadily and began circling again; Graffius resumed stalking him.

That established the pattern of the fight, which surprisingly lasted the full six rounds. Graffius toiled through Vega's increasingly desperate punches, never hurrying, never altering his approach, never acting as if he knew he could knock Vega out by hitting him twice instead of once. Vega, for his part, weathered blows that seemed to be leaving craters in his head and body. He aged visibly, changing with the knowledge of what he would have to endure to last out the fight. He learned to recognize the click as Graffius got his spacing in order, and to duck forward under the arc of the overhand right, but then Graffius, who had hurt his right hand, switched to left hooks and belted him just as hard with those. Vega was down again in the fourth and fifth rounds but he went the distance, to great applause. Each time he went down it seemed to be the end — in the fourth, especially, when he crashed puppetlike on his side — but each time he hoisted himself up and wearily resumed moving and feeling for the beat that preceded Graffius's next bomb.

Even though the fight resembled the demolition of a building more than a contest of equals, it was never impossible to imagine Vega finding a way to cope with Graffius. The click presented Vega a key to the limitations of Graffius's style. If in a rematch Vega learned to disturb the puncher's balance by jabbing just when Graffius paused before launching (Holmes, sitting at ringside, could show him how to do it), and if Graffius never learned to throw combinations, Vega might well win. As it turned out, both men hung up the gloves after a few more fights, and Vega never got a chance to even the score in a rematch. Perhaps neither one was ever better in the ring than he was during their encounter. Still, the evening held a lesson for Vega to consider, if he chose to, bound up with the shame and hurt of a public beating in front of a hometown crowd.

*   *   *

Holmes vs. Harris
Heavyweights. 10 rounds.
July 29, 1997. New York, N.Y.

An hour after the main event was over, as security men herded out stragglers and as a cleanup crew raised echoes in The Theater at Madison Square Garden, Larry Holmes sat on a folding chair and talked shop. His voice had lost most of the touchy, suspicious edges that normally animate his interviews; all the energy he had spent and the blows he had taken that evening had worn it smooth, almost tender. He was saying that he and his wife, Diane, who was sitting next to him, came into New York to do business: he had a fight at the Garden; she bought stock for the lingerie store she owned in Easton. Holmes said, "I like to come with her, buy some lingerie." His audience of male reporters laughed nervously, but he insisted, smiling, "No, I mean it, man. It's business. I like doing it." They had converged on Holmes in a half circle, craning forward to take notes and yearningly stretching microphones toward him like officers attending a general in one of those big nineteenth-century battle paintings. Their laughter managed to communicate both eager respect and a certain impatience to steer Holmes back toward familiar territory: *So, champ, did the kid ever hurt you?*

Holmes looked all of his forty-seven years. He had gone ten rounds with Maurice Harris, a twenty-two-year-old of moderate accomplishments who had hit him often and with feeling. Holmes's nose and eyes had the ripe, dewy look that indicates fresh punishment. There had been a moment near the end of the fifth round when Holmes, jarred by a right hand, looked hurt, but in his long career he had learned to gather and manage himself until his legs return to him, which they did in this case. Even if Harris had not shaken Holmes's redoubtable self-possession, the almost universal ringside consensus when the final bell rang was that Harris had carried at least six rounds and deserved the victory. The judges, however, awarded a split decision to Holmes. After their verdict was announced, and as good-natured boos rolled down from the largely pro-Holmes crowd, everyone tried to figure out if the judges had been swayed by Holmes's hard right hands to the body, by his impressive aura, or (as the more conspiracy-minded suggested to their neighbors) by a deal supposedly being cooked up to match him against George Foreman in a big-money battle.

Holmes now hit less and got hit more than in the past. Watching him wait and wait to throw a punch, his partisans twisted in their seats and became short of breath as he let openings in his opponent's defense present themselves only to close up again, unexploited. But he was not a figure of pathos. If he had passed the point at which he might learn anything new in the ring (other than that he had slipped even further from his bygone prime since the last time he had fought), he had deep reserves of experience on which to draw. There was something wise and elegant in his movements as he pursued Harris around the ring, something that said, "Don't go far, son, I've got a beating to give

you." Reflecting on the fight, Holmes regretted that he
hadn't been able to administer the beating in full, and he
acknowledged it was a close contest that could have been
awarded to either man, but he felt no anguish about the
tainted victory. Judges had snatched away from him much
bigger fights — most famously the two controversial title
bouts against Michael Spinks that broke Holmes's string of
forty-eight victories without a defeat — and he was confident that he deserved finally to win a close one. "A hard
day at the office," he called it, and seemed satisfied to take
his bruises and his money home to Easton and leave it at
that.

Harris, of course, was not at all satisfied. He had left earlier, an angry red mark under his left eye, after telling the
clustered reporters that he had been robbed. As Harris told
it, the judges had pitied a doddering Holmes. "The man
was slow, you know?" he said. "Slow and old. He only
landed about three jabs that I could count that were flush
in the whole fight." The young man was feeling the double
hurt of hard punches and an opportunity unjustly lost.
Faithfully mimicking Holmes's defensive rigor and long
jabs, turning himself into a younger and smaller Holmes in
a triumph of autodidacticism under fire, Harris had outboxed a heavyweight all-timer. Growing more confident as
Holmes tired, Harris had felt himself coming of age as a
fighter and building a rosier moneymaking future, but
when the fight was over the judges took it away from him.
His transformative moment had come to nothing, and perhaps he already knew that he would never again come that

close to breaking through. (After losing to Holmes and then to three contenders, he would recede from discussions of heavyweights who mattered.) Harris had a right to be aggrieved, but it seemed ungracious to fault Holmes for being old, as opposed to accusing the judges of being blind or crooked.

Once Holmes left there was no reason to stay. It was past midnight. Outside the Garden, there was a small knot of fans around Floyd Patterson, who had been interrupted while getting into his car, which was running at the curb with the door open. Still trim in his sixties and sporting his old flattop haircut with the little flip in front, he patiently signed the proffered scraps of paper. At the time, Patterson chaired the New York State Athletic Commission; soon he would be obliged to step down from that post because his memory and other mental functions had become seriously impaired. A hardworking, smallish heavyweight champion who fought on well past his prime, Patterson took his share of beatings, most notably from Ingemar Johansson, Sonny Liston, and Muhammad Ali. He carried decades of hurt with a straight-backed, courtly air of decency, perhaps all that was left of his celebrated passion for perfecting his body and his fighting craft. As the fans around his car dispersed, the last of them said, "Good night, Mr. Patterson." The chairman smiled, asked them to please call him Floyd, and said good night in the gentlest voice heard in or near the Garden that night.

Acknowledgments

THIS BOOK'S corner has been crowded with learned trainers, astute managers, and deft cutpersons.

I owe a special debt of gratitude to Larry Holmes, the sensei of Easton, and to the crew of masters and apprentices at his gym. There and elsewhere, so many boxers, cornermen, promoters, reporters, judges, commissioners, and other fight people have been so generous to me with their time and ideas that I must take refuge in thanking them collectively. Some of their names appear in the book, so I can at least append silent thanks wherever they do. Bob Trieger, Jay Newman, and Rita Apicelli, whose names do not appear elsewhere in the book, have been going out of their way to help me for years.

Eamon Dolan, an old-school editor in the very best sense, tied the manuscript's ankles together with a short string to improve its footwork. Larry Cooper unflinchingly applied the chilled steel to its swollen eye. They are the latest in a line of editors who have expertly helped me work at writing about boxing, among them David Rowell, Anne Fadiman, Kelefa Sanneh, Mike Vazquez, Rob Odom, Toby Lester, and Anna Marie Murphy. Susan Rabiner, a hard-boiled agent with the soul of an editor, was especially wise in her matchmaking.

I have relied on the opinions and goodwill of Charles Cherington, Chris Erikson, Mike Ezra, and Gary Moser, all of whom read the manuscript in its entirety, and Bobby McDermut, who remembered what I had forgotten. Mike and Gary got into a terrifically erudite e-mail argument about whether Sandy Saddler could be described as "no aesthetician." Finally I had to cut the phrase; it would have required a page-long footnote.

I have also relied on the strength and wisdom of my parents, Salvatore and Pilar Rotella, and my brothers, Sebastian and Sal; on Lola Klein for time and Peter Klein for space; and on Tina Klein, as always, for everything. And Ling-li Rotella relied on me, which made writing a book seem like honest work.